# Monies in Societies

*"What is money? Money doesn't say it's money. People
who see it say it's money."*

# Monies in Societies

## Walter C. Neale
The University of Tennessee

 **Chandler & Sharp Publishers, Inc.**

San Francisco

**Chandler & Sharp Series in
Cross-Cultural Themes**

GENERAL EDITOR

Douglass R. Price-Williams
  *University of California, Los Angeles*

CONSULTING EDITORS
L. L. Langness
Robert B. Edgerton
  *both University of California, Los Angeles*

**Library of Congress Cataloging in Publication Data**

Neale, Walter C        1925-
  Monies in societies.

  (Chandler & Sharp series in cross-cultural themes)
  Bibliography: p.
  Includes index.
  1. Money—History.      I. Title.      II. Series.
HG231.N37        332.4'9        76-519
ISBN 0-88316-525-2

INTERNATIONAL STANDARD BOOK NUMBER  0-88316-525-2

LIBRARY OF CONGRESS CATALOG CARD NO.  76-519

PRINTED IN THE UNITED STATES OF AMERICA


Book Design: Joseph M. Roter
Composition: Hansen & Associates Graphics

# CONTENTS

# ACKNOWLEDGMENTS

A number of friends and relations, of varying ages, experiences, and interest, from students in mathematics to professors in economics and anthropology, read a draft of the manuscript and responded with all sorts of comments, most of which led to changes (and all of which led to worrying). To them I owe a great many improvements in the argument and presentation, and to all I am grateful for encouragement and especially for courage. They are J. Adams, G. Asthana, K. Brown, K. H. Bruckner, J. Campen, G. Dalton, W. C. Gordon, A. H. Keally, R. Kyle, M. J. Leaf, H. H. Liebhafsky, A. Mayhew, C. S. Neale, J. S. Neale, P. A. C. Neale, G. Sirkin, C. C. Thompson, and J. F. Wilson.

Also, I am indebted to Professor Douglass Price-Williams and his unknown readers for suggestions, and to Mssrs. Howard Chandler and Jonathan Sharp for clarity in their responses and cooperation in crises. Mr. W. L. Parker's editing and questioning did much to clarify the presentation and it was an unusual pleasure to work with a person so adept at improving one's work without altering one's style or outlook.

To my colleague Anne Mayhew I owe the most. So much has she been involved in thinking out the argument, in editing each draft, in interpreting readers' comments, and in suggesting solutions to problems, that she should perhaps be listed as co-author. In fact, she has contributed so much that she too should be held responsible for any errors remaining in the book.

# Monies in Societies

# I

## ABOUT MONIES

If one had a time machine to rove world history, one would see an enormous variety of things being passed from one person to another: television sets, yams, cowrie shells, cows, rubies, books, metal bars and discs, chickens, and rectangular slips of paper with printing and script on them, sometimes also pictures and numbers. The different kinds of things which one could record in a very long lifetime would probably exceed a million. Some of the things would be handed over with joy, some with tears; sometimes the transactions would be accompanied with great ceremony, sometimes with violence, sometimes with apparent indifference. A time-and-space traveler might classify the items in his long list: some as subsistence goods, some as luxury goods, a third kind as treasured items, a fourth as tools and machines, a fifth as animals, a sixth as lucky charms, a seventh as sacred items, and so on. One very likely class into which he would fit some items would be "money."

Why does a person report that disc-shaped stones (with holes in their centers to permit carrying them) were a money on the island of Yap? Why do others say that shells strung on strings are money on Pacific islands? Why do people report pigs on New Guinea and surrounding islands as money? Cattle in Africa? Wampum among American Indians? Slave girls in fifth-century Ireland? Silk in China? Tobacco in colonial Maryland and Virginia? Furs in Russia and among American Indians? Mats and cloths of bark on Pacific islands, in Africa, and among Indians of the American northwest? Cowrie shells in Bengal, in west and east Africa, in China, and in many other places? Brass rods, copper wire, and iron hoes in Africa? And so on through an ever-lengthening list?

Why are all these things called money? Why, by contrast, does no one call

1

television sets and books money, even though they pass from one person to another? There is not one answer, but there are a limited number. In each case the item called money was used in at least one of the following ways: (1) as a means of payment; (2) as a medium of exchange; (3) as a standard of value; (4) as a store of value (or wealth); (5) as a standard of deferred payment (a way of expressing a debt to be paid in the future); or (6) as a unit of account. Although some reported monies appear to have all these functions, others appear to have had only one, or two, or three of them. Furthermore, different monies have been limited in respect of the kinds of payment for which they could be used; limited in respect of the kinds of things or events they could value (standard); limited in the kinds of things they could buy (medium of exchange); and limited in respect of who in the society could use them.

Our modern money is unusual (but not unique) in being used in all six ways and in the wide range of things and services it can buy, the wide range of things and performances we evaluate in terms of our money. Almost all material things which we use in everyday life we can buy or sell, and many performances—what we call services—can be bought or sold. In fact, most things and services which we use can be got *only* by the payment of money. The use of land for agriculture, industry, commerce, and housing requires payment of a purchase price or a rent in money. The raw materials, power, and labor which go into producing the goods and services we use must all be bought for money. However, in modern industrialized societies it is rare to be able to buy privileges or immunities. Two centuries ago one could, if acceptable to the regiment, buy a commission in the British army. Today it is difficult as well as illegal to buy elective office, national honors, forgiveness for crime, or high grades in school. Appointments to the House of Lords (rudely called "beer baronies") and some United States ambassadorships have been indirectly purchased, or so some say—but certainly not directly and publicly bought. When a performance which we ought not to buy is purchased, we call the transaction "bribery and corruption."

We can get money to buy things only by selling something we own, by selling the use of something we own (including our labor time), or by borrowing (or begging, or stealing) money. When we lack money we starve to death or else die first of exposure—or we would, were it not for food stamps and the Salvation Army. (No wonder a friend once told me: "You economists don't know what money is: money is canned freedom.") So great is dependence on money in capitalist societies that many farmers would be unable to eat, clothe themselves, or build houses without the money they receive from the sales of their specialized products. We also express and pay taxes and fines in money. We evaluate much of the cost of wars in money; we express the size of our national output of goods and services in money.

Because our modern money buys so much, is needed for so many things, measures so much, serves so many functions, it has been called "all-purpose" or "general-purpose" money in contrast to the "limited-purpose" monies of many other societies. It might perhaps be better to call it "multipurpose" money, as a reminder of the limits upon the uses even of our money, while retaining the contrast with monies far more limited in functions and uses.

No effort to define money will satisfy enough people to be a success. This is true because we include a lot of ideas—about the functions and characteristics or traits of money—in our general concept of money. In one place, particular things (or ways of using things) that have moneyish functions or characteristics will not have all the functions and characteristics which we associate with the idea of money. In another place a very similar thing will not have any moneyish functions at all (consider the similarity between a coin and a commemorative medal). "What is money really?" is a question like "What is government really?" or "What is politics really?" Such questions are hard to investigate. There are some core ideas in government—power, and its acquisition and use; legitimate authority; laws and ruling; public as opposed to private—but the systems we might call "government" or "political" vary immensely. There are political or governmental aspects to many institutions in our society: corporations have been called "private governments"; some would say the exercise of power by a parent punishing a child is political; people talk of office politics and departmental politics. In contrast there are systems that lack any institutions or processes clearly like our government and politics: for instance, there is a book on African systems called *Tribes Without Rulers*[1] (but they certainly were not tribes without rules and processes and ways of handling disputes). Colonial administrations often had trouble differentiating "big men" (powerful, important, admired, wealthy) from "chiefs" and "headmen" (exercising legitimate governmental authority).

And so it is with money: we have a number of core ideas about functions and traits, but there is no clearer an answer to "What is money?" than there is to "What is government?" Of course, we all know, at least in a general way, what is meant by "the government of the United States" or "the government of Pennsylvania" or "the government of Japan." And we know what is meant, again in a general way, by "American money" or "British money." But just as the United States, British, and Indian governments differ in important respects, so too do the monetary systems of the United States, Britain, and India. As the United States, British, and Japanese political systems have enough in common to call them "responsible democracies," so too do their monetary systems have enough in common to say that they all use "modern multipurpose monies."

It is best, therefore, to think of money as a classification of functions,

---

[1] John Middleton and David Tait, *Tribes Without Rulers*.

traits, and processes, some of which are prominent in one society, others in another; and to recognize that there are "societies without money." Just as we say that there are "governmental aspects" to large corporations without meaning that "General Motors is a government just like the government of India," so also should we be able to say of systems which have something in common with our modern money that they are "moneyish" or have "limited-purpose monies" without meaning that they are just like our monetary system or even importantly like it.

Furthermore, since all monies are *parts of larger systems* of economic and social relationships, a money should always be thought about in terms of its functions, purposes, and *consequences within a particular system*. A vote in the United States House of Representatives is political; a vote in the House of Commons is political; but the consequences of the votes may be different for the functioning of the American and British governments. A cow in Texas passes from one owner to another in a money transaction; a cow in Kenya changes ownership in payment—but the purpose, functions, and consequences of the two transactions are very different.

## Obligation, Debt, and Payment

It is difficult to talk about money without calling to mind the ideas of obligation, debt, and payment. In any society there are obligations of one person (or organization) to another which arise as results of the actions of people. The ways in which obligations can arise are many indeed: from parentage, from contracts (express or implied), from commission of a crime, from omission of the performance of a duty, from undertaking a particular role (father, president), or from luck (drawing the short straw or holding the right lottery ticket). There is also enormous variety in the kinds of obligations and the ways in which the obligations can be fulfilled. Within a society the conditions for fulfillment will vary depending on the kind of obligation and on how it arose. What are apparently the same kind of obligation in different societies can call for quite different kinds of performance in fulfilling the obligation, and kinds of obligations can arise in some societies which have no apparent counterparts in other societies. All that is universal is that obligations must be fulfilled or there will be some kind of "chop." (The kinds of pressures to conform are many, and an anthropologist friend has suggested the general concept of the "chop" to embrace all "negative reinforcements" of proper behavior.)

The ideas of "obligation," or "debt," and of "payment" overlap but are not identical; and the obligations we would call debts and the fulfillments we would call payments vary from society to society. In our society, obligations we commonly think of as debts often arise from a contract calling for payment in money, or from failure to deliver goods or to perform a service, but we need not have a contract (express or implied) to be put under an obligation which we would call a debt. For instance, the obligation to pay an income tax to the government arises out of the receipt of income. It is a consequence of earning, or of owning earning assets, within the nation's boundaries. An obligation to pay money to a county government arises out of the act of speeding (and the policeman's act of catching the speeder and the judge's act of fining the culprit). An obligation to pay a woman a monthly sum in alimony arises out of the actions of husband and/or wife in getting a divorce and the judge's decision about how much an ex-husband should pay. All these are obligations that are fulfilled by the payment of money. Although taxes, fines, and alimony are not commercial in origin nor contractual in nature, in our system they do affect our ability to purchase goods and services or to influence the allocation of productive resources to different uses, and hence they affect the everyday functioning of our economy. But an obligation need not involve the payment of a thing (that is, be a debt); it may or it may not arise from activities of a commercial or otherwise economic nature; its fulfillment may or may not have important consequences for the production and distribution of the world's wherewithals. Some examples will illustrate the range:

The obligations of the medieval serf were importantly economic but not commercial; they arose from the "accident" of birth. An obligation to fight for and advise an overlord arose from the pledge of fealty by a knight or baron to his lord (a kind of contract). In the medieval city an obligation to work for a master arose from the action of a parent in apprenticing his child to the master. In ancient Greece (and in a great many other places—see Sir Walter Scott's "The Lady of the Lake") an obligation to supply hospitality and protection to someone from abroad arose if one had received hospitality from that person. In a great many places an obligation to feed, clothe, and protect a child arises from the act of living with the child's mother.

There are various ways in which obligations can be fulfilled. There are lifelong obligations like the service owed by a knight to his overlord. Other obligations end with some event not within the control of the obliged person, as is the case with a parent's obligation toward his child when the child reaches maturity. Still others can be fulfilled—ended—by an act. It is these latter sorts, especially those which we end by paying money, that we often think of as "debts." The fulfillment of some debt obligations by an act can permanently end the relationship between parties. Thus when I have finished paying the contracted amount on my house mortgage I need have no further dealings with the mortgage company, nor the company with me. A large number of obligations arising in our society are ended almost before one realizes one has incurred an obligation: one pays for groceries in a store almost simultaneously with becoming indebted for them.

Some obligations by their very fulfillment give rise to further obligations between the parties. In systems of gift and countergift, the "payment" by the "indebted" party relieves him of the debt but simultaneously obliges the payee to make a payment in the future. Whereas in our society a debt arising from bagging the onions at the store and going to the cashier is paid immediately in money, a debt arising from "borrowing" onions from a neighbor is paid only when the neighbor wants something—most unlikely to be onions—later on. And that repayment—in cat food, perhaps—will be phrased not as a repayment but as another borrowing which will both reverse and continue the relationship.

In western society we usually mean "owing money" when we use the word debt, but we do also use the word in other contexts ("I am forever indebted to you for your kindnesses"). Payment usually means "paying money" for a good or service, but we "pay for our crimes," feed the neighbor's cat in payment for the coffee she lent us, and "pay through the nose" for social errors.

Differences in obligations and their fulfillment are strikingly illustrated when we compare two cases of willful killing. In the United States a willful killing obliges the killer to serve time in prison ("paying a debt to society," we call it). However, consider the many societies in which there are blood feuds. In some of these societies the "blood debt" can be paid by the killer or his relatives transferring valuables (such as cows, cowries, and pigs) to the relatives of the victim. And in these cases the debt is paid to the victim's relatives, not "to society."

Obligation, debt, and payment are closely associated ideas. We have come to think of money in our commercial and capitalist society as the usual (but not exclusive) means of payment, and hence have our feeling that, somehow, money, payment, and debt (and obligation) constitute an interrelated whole. Therefore, when we see people in another culture handing over anything to liquidate an obligation or to acquire a power or privilege, we are inclined to call it money. Calling such anythings "money" is not wrong, but presents dangers to accurate understanding: the dangers of assuming that payments are commercial or economic in origin or nature; and, more importantly, of assuming that the *consequences* of the payment are similar in other societies to the consequences that follow in our own.

Economists have assumed close relationships between money, debt, and payment. They have tried to describe or to define money in terms of its traits and functions, drawing largely on the nature and roles of money in our western, industrialized economies during the last century or two. The next two sections of this chapter outline how economists and students of money have analyzed its functions and characterized its traits, and show the logical relationships among these functions and traits.

## Functions of Money

Economists have often said that money has four closely related functions: medium of exchange, standard of value, store of value, and standard of deferred payment. *Medium of exchange* means that money is received in payment for a good sold or a service rendered and is later used to purchase a good or a service. As a *medium,* money is a way-station in the exchange of goods or services sold or rendered for goods or services purchased. This function has been expressed in the formulation "Goods into Money into Goods," meaning that in this function money is but an intermediate, convenient stage in converting one kind of good into another. In the sale the money is equated with the good or service sold; in the purchase the money is equated with the good or service purchased. It has thus served as a *standard of value* for each good (or service) sold and purchased. In the time between sale and purchase the medium thus served automatically as a *store of value.* Since the medium thus already serves as a standard of value and a store of value, it is an obvious choice to express promises to pay in the future in the same units, thus making money a standard of *deferred payment.* When a notation is made about money as a standard of value or as a standard of deferred payment, or when any other record is made of a money valuation or transaction, money is often called a *unit of account.*

In this century money has often been called "purchasing power," a phrase which highlights the fact that the holder of money has the ability to command goods and services or to refrain from commanding them—the power inherent in having money. "Purchasing power" implies the older functions: purchasing power acquired by a sale becomes a medium of exchange; in purchasing, one establishes a value of the thing bought (standard of value); holding the power to purchase is to store value; and so money is still an obvious choice for expressing the value (the standard by which to judge the sufficiency) of what is promised to be paid in the future (deferred payment).

All of these functions can be derived from the idea of money as a *means of payment.* Money serves as a medium of exchange when the payment to a seller for services rendered or goods sold is thereafter used by the seller-become-buyer to pay for what he buys. When a future obligation is expressed in money terms, money serves as a standard of deferred payment. The act of equating a money payment with the thing paid for makes money a standard of value. When the means to make payment are hoarded, money serves as a store of value. The recording of payments past or to be made in the future makes money a unit of account.

The idea of "means of payment" has the virtue, also, that is embraces payments which are not clearly made in the process of current or future exchanges—such payments as fines, taxes, and gifts. Each such payment *can* be called an exchange. One can say that fines are an exchange of "your money for your freedom." Similarly, taxes can be called an exchange of money for public goods; and gifts, the exchange of money for love or for an easier conscience. But such uses of "exchange" do stretch normal meaning for no reason other than to defend the position that "money is really a medium of exchange."

## Traits of Money

One important trait is that money is *quantifiable* in a system of small gradations. In this respect money is like a system of weights or of measures. Money is also *fungible*. That is, any one unit, or several units, of a money is substitutable for any other units of the same "value" or denomination in the monetary system. Four quarters and a dollar bill are "the same" for monetary purposes (not for flipping coins), as are two five-dollar bills and a ten-dollar bill. In this way also money is like the systems of weights and measures: twelve inches are as good as a foot. If you offered me four of your bubblegum cards for my seashell, I would almost certainly ask "Which cards?" and add, "No Washington Redskins." But if you offered me fifty cents I would not ask "Which fifty cents?" Rather, I would say simply "Yes" or "No" or "Maybe, let me think." The question "Which fifty cents?" would be silly, so fungible has our money become.

Other traits associated with money have been durability, portability, divisibility, recognizability—traits which obviously refer to the stuffs (material) of which monies are made. The traits were used to explain why metals were used (metal lasts almost forever, easily divides into small bits, and one can test it for purity). These traits are also associated with the functions of money. Durability is needed for a store of value. Portability is desirable in a medium of exchange (who wants to drag elephant carcasses around?), as is divisibility since the amount required to pay for different purchases varies so much. And, of course, one wants to know, to recognize easily, that it is money one is getting. But, as will become apparent, the physical traits of durability, portability, divisibility, and recognizability are not essential to a money, which in fact may not be made of a stuff at all but "made of promises" (see Chapter VI).

## Money: Logic vs. History

It is important always to bear in mind that the relationships among the functions of money are *logical* and *not* historical ones. Evidence on the historical origins of some monies is sparse, on the origins of other monies nonexistent. There is no historical evidence to make us believe that one function came first in time and that the others followed. Despite the fact that many a text on money says that money originated in the inconveniences of barter, that money was invented as a medium of exchange, or that a good commonly used in trade gradually evolved into a medium of exchange—

despite such statements, neither historical evidence nor argument by analogy from contemporary nonliterate societies lends support to this speculative history.

What has just been said is not to deny that the logical connections among the functions of money are there for people to make: that when a money is used in one or two ways, people *may* realize they can use it in other ways. Its usefulness for many purposes may be recognized and the money *may* acquire all the functions and uses that we associate with money. But while such a result is possible, it does not seem to have been a common course of events. Rather, the limited use of monies in various societies shows that a money does not necessarily *or even usually* acquire all the functions and uses we associate with money. In fact, it is necessary to deny emphatically that a money with one or more functions in one specific socioeconomic system has or will take on all the other functions in and consequences for that system which our money has in and for our system. Neither can one assume that our money has all the functions and consequences that some other money may some day have, or that our money serves all the purposes that have been served by other monies.

Subsequent chapters will describe and analyze the differing natures and roles of monies in a variety of social systems. They will show how some monies are used in payment but not as media of exchange, how other monies are used in only a few kinds of exchange, and how a money can be the important standard of value but not the important means of payment.

## Treasure, Utility, and Money

In functions and in the specific uses to which they are put, treasured items overlap with money, and either a treasured item or a money may have other, utilitarian uses. However, treasuring or usefulness does not make something money, nor need money stuffs be treasured or useful.

Around the world and through the ages one finds treasured items: things which people strive to acquire, which once acquired they strive to keep, which they admire, and which are turned over to others as gifts or as payments. Such things are valued because they are considered beautiful, because they are believed to have magical or supernatural powers, because they have sentimental associations, or because they can be turned over to others at some future time for some economic, religious, political, or social purpose. The hoard of Tutankhamen, the Sistine Chapel, a Rubens painting, a Victoria Cross in a regimental mess—all are treasures. So are hoards of gold and silver, and so also are cows for many Africans, who can recognize each animal in a herd *and* remember its genealogy through many generations.

In our society jewels are treasured. They appear in finger rings and earrings, bracelets, necklaces, and tiaras. Typically the giving and receiving of treasured jewels is associated with marriage (and/or sexual access) and the wearing and keeping of jewels is associated with women. Barring diamonds for industrial cutting and occasional other uses of jewels, there is no everyday use for them other than keeping/showing/storing them. They prove wealth, beauty, and the love of the giver. They are also, certainly, stores of value. They can be sold—converted into purchasing power and so into other forms of wealth or beauty or utility or power. From the individual's point of view the store-of-value function of a diamond or a ruby is clear: she can sell it when she wants and historically the price of jewels has remained high and appears (at least to many) to rise in terms of the prices of other goods.

Some monies are made of stuffs which are themselves treasured: gold and silver are the obvious cases. Some treasured items also serve money uses: shells and feathers in Oceania. Other treasured items do not: paintings are highly valued, may serve as a store of value, but otherwise have no money uses, and are not thought of as money. Some treasured items which are not thought of as money are easily exchanged for money, while others have little value in exchange for money: for instance, a diamond ring can easily be sold for money, but little money will be offered for somebody else's Medal of Honor. Some things with utility may also be treasured, such as out-of-print books, yet not serve as money. Other things which we say are "invaluable" or "beyond price" are greatly treasured, yet we will not give them values in money because we fear that any exchange value put on one may understate its value in some better-run world.

Some items are treasured, used as money, and have utilitarian employments. In many African cultures cattle are highly valued and circulate as counterpayment for a wife and as payment in compensation of bodily injury or death (called bloodwealth, or wergeld). Within these specific systems cattle-as-treasure make sense: one must acquire cattle for payment of bloodwealth or bridewealth (but there are societies in which women move from one household to another without prepayment and in which there are sanctions other than the requirement that bridewealth be returned to stabilize domestic relations; and there are also societies with both bridewealth and little stability of marriage). At the same time that the cattle are treasured they are also of daily use for milk and blood, at their death for hides and meat, and where arable farming and livestock keeping are mixed, for their manure. From "the outside"—given the different perceptions and beliefs of another society—it is often hard to see why an item is treasured, is used as money, or is not used as money. From "the inside"—that is, given the functioning social system and its members' beliefs and expectations—the roles of treasured items make sense.

The sometimes close overlapping of money uses with treasuring and with the utility of things may confuse our thinking about money. One danger is assuming that because a treasure is a store of value it has other money uses; or because it is occasionally used in payment, it has other money uses. Another danger is assuming that a treasure is a store of value or means of payment: it may not be if the treasured aspect is specifically limited to one or a few people or uses, as is the case with medals, national monuments, or sacred objects usable only by a priestly caste in religious ceremonies.

A third danger lies in trying to explain a money by its treasured or utilitarian traits—the guesswork use of "because." Cattle are used in limited-purpose payments, are stores of value, and are a standard of value in Africa, where they are useful but not clearly more useful than on a Texas ranch where all income depends on the sale of the cattle. Copper wires are used in payment and as a store of value in west Africa, but copper wires are far more useful in any electrical device in a developed society where they are neither means of payment nor standard of value. (Our copper pennies have been worth far more as monetary units than they have been as metal, although in the 1970s, since copper is becoming more highly valued as a metal, it may disappear from our means of payment, as silver did a few years ago.) There are no universal rules for relating value, treasure, utility, and money uses: what appears to be a reasonable relationship in one place or time turns out to be wrong in another. Treasure is as it is admired; utility is as a thing is done with; and money is as it serves moneyish functions. None of these aspects necessarily explains any of the others.

# II

## MONEY: STUFF, IDEA, AND PROCESS

The word "money" has at least three distinct uses. Money may refer to a *stuff*—an actual physical item—which is used to make payments. Money may also be an *idea* we use in comparing the values of two things or events, to add together dissimilar items by expressing them in the common denominator of money values, or to express an obligation in a money value. Thirdly, money may refer to a *process* by which obligations are liquidated, debts paid, or promises fulfilled.

### Money as Stuff

Money as stuff is the common use of the word *money*, the use we all learn as children. It is illustrated by the paying of obligations with coins, in Africa with cows or cowries, among some Pacific islanders with pigs, or with strings of feathers or polished shells. Such use of the word is what has led us to speak of "silver money," "cattle money," "shell money." The danger in speaking in such a manner is that one is all too apt to assume, perhaps without really thinking about the matter, that these monies all serve essentially the same purposes, that their existence has the same effects in all societies—in short, to assume that the important differences among them are only the different stuffs of which they are made. But this is not, of course, the case: different uses of different monies in different societies have different effects; and not all monies are made of a stuff.

### Money as Idea

Spoken or written symbols express valuations made in the money: the quotation of a price or the record of a debt. But as a standard of value a money

need have no physical embodiment, just as many other systems of measurement have no physical embodiment—the nautical mile exists only as a mental
construct or concept resulting from the process of "shooting" the sun or stars
in navigating. The dollars in "$1.4 trillion" of United States gross national
product exist only as ideas, and are about as comprehensible, or incompre-
hensible, as "light years." The statement is not even about dollars: it is about
an immensely varied bunch of goods and services produced in a year—about
millions of packages of frozen spinach and about miles of interstate highways
built and about rub-downs in massage parlors. It is a statement about "how
much" such a collection of things and events amounts to and such a statement
can be made only by measuring each in the common denominator of money
values and summing the values.

The statement "I have $473 in my bank account" is not a statement about
any *things* in my bank. It is a statement about how much, expressed in money
terms, the bank is obligated to pay as I order: it is a statement about a debt.
This is my reason for using, throughout this book, the terms "at a bank" or
"with a bank" whenever speaking of deposits or depositing: there is little
except records of promises *in* the bank.

We also use money as a standard of value to express judgments and make
comparisons, real or metaphorical: "It isn't worth the three bucks." "He
never learned the value of a dollar." "It's cheaper to pay a fine once in a while
than to pay a parking fee every day." "I wouldn't give a red cent for your
opinion." Or, "A good woman is beyond price." Such statements as these
convey meaning or attitude, using the vocabulary of a system or standard of
measurement. They refer to money in a way analogous to the way we use the
system of linear measurements when we say "Five foot ten isn't tall enough to
play basketball" or "You'll need another four feet of rope to do that." The
"three bucks" and the "red cent" are in the heads of the speaker and listener,
ideas of value derived from experience in getting and spending money, just as
the 5'10" of height) and the 4' (of rope) are ideas about length derived from
being told how tall people are and from using rulers and tape measures.

Often, when making statements about values or future payments, money-
as-a-standard is associated with a particular money stuff, using the word
which names the stuff to serve as the name of the unit expressing the measure
of value. But people can talk about values and obligations in terms of a stuff
without actually using the stuff.

In the African cattle cultures negotiations about the bridewealth to be
handed over as part of a marriage arrangement are expressed in numbers of
cattle. Cattle, however, may not be handed over, but instead the actual
payment may be made, at least in part, in goats or in iron. In medieval Europe
contracts would be expressed in pounds, shillings, and pence but the payment

would sometimes be made in saddles or goats or other goods.[1] In ancient Mesopotamia obligations were expressed in weights of silver (there were no coins) but payments would be made in barley or oil. In the American South after the Civil War, many country stores expressed the value of goods supplied to sharecroppers in dollars, and the value of cotton delivered to the store in dollars, but actual payment by the sharecroppers was in cotton delivered to the storekeeper. Similarly in company towns the company store expressed values in dollars and took payment in company scrip or in debits against wages expressed in dollars, but no silver or paper dollars changed hands.

"Money" as used in these cases was a standard of value or a numerical statement about an obligation in terms of the standard. The standard was expressed in real-stuff words but the actual transactions were completed, the obligations liquidated, in terms of some other stuff (or in terms of the labor of the employee, expressed in but not paid in the current money of the country).

## Money as Process

Handing the cashier three pennies for the after-dinner mint is a process of paying and requires stuff (copper pennies). If, however, one can act, and can get other people to act, in such a way that the set of obligations among the people involved is changed, and if all are satisfied that payment has been made, then one would have a *process* of payment without any money stuff. A series of events that puts each participant in a different legal position is a process, not a thing. A process may involve the manipulation of a thing but that does not make a specific manipulation of the thing essential to the process, or to achieve the desired results. For instance, in American courts it is common for an officer of the court to hold out a Bible and for the witness to put his hand on the Bible and "swear" to tell the truth—with the legal consequence that, if he is caught lying, he can be sent to jail for the crime of perjury, But a Bible, let alone the specific physical traits of the copy, is not necessary to turn plain lies into criminal perjuries. The result is the same if the witness holds up a hand and "affirms" that he will tell the truth.

The bulk of modern money—the "demand deposits" (checking accounts) in commercial banks—is not a thing, not a stuff at all, but is a set of legally binding statements about rights and obligations. A demand deposit is a promise by the bank to pay the depositor, or whomever the depositor orders the bank to pay, in a form satisfactory to the payee. There is no stuff in the bank corresponding to the demand deposit (the promise of the bank). Payment is made by reducing the amount promised to the check-writing

---

[1]Carlo M. Cipolla, *Money, Prices, and Civilization in the Mediterranean World, Fifth to Seventeenth Century*, pp. 3-12.

depositor and increasing the amount promised to the recipient (payee) of the check, at the same or at a different bank.

To own a demand deposit is to have the right, the legal power, to act so as to set in motion a series of events that will alter the state of legal rights and obligations, including the rights (demand deposits) and obligations (debts, payments owing) of the owner. The transactions involved are best called a process because the check I write to the store, deposited by the store at its bank, sets in train a number of actions: people in the store's bank make a notation of more money promised to the store in the bank's books; they bundle the check up with other checks to send to the clearing house; people in the clearing house total the checks received; they pass my check on to my bank where people make a notation of less money promised to me; and then they bundle my checks up every month and return them to me with a statement about how much the bank thinks it still owes me. No thing—no stuff—other than the check, *which is an order to pay,* has passed in payment. The actions of myself in writing the check, of the store in depositing the check, of the banks' employees in accepting and recording the passage of the check—these actions change the legal obligations existing among the participants. I no longer am obligated (in debt) to the store; the store's bank is more obligated (owes more) to the store; my bank is less obligated (owes less) to me. The records will prove that the actions occurred and the courts will enforce the new state of obligations (debts and credits). It is the actions taken—the processes of banking, with their legal consequences—that have "paid my debt." No stuff has been paid (handed over). In fact, a peculiarity of our system of payment by *process* in the banking system is that the only movable stuff—the check—returns at the end of the process to the payer. What "backs" a system of demand deposits is no *thing* but a process: the enforcement of our law of contract. The demand deposit is a legally binding contract, and will be enforced by the courts. As is the case with most contracts, fulfillment of the promise in the contract seldom requires the intervention of the courts. (At this point I think I had best ask the reader who feels that "there must be some stuff somewhere in all this"—that I have just described a system so unlikely as to be impossible—to suspend his disbelief until he has read Chapter VI, "Promises, Promises, Nothing but Promises." That chapter discusses the relationships among demand deposits, bank assets, checks, and payments by banks.)

## Stuff-as-Stuff and Stuff-as-Evidence

As children we learned to associate money with a stuff, and there is much in the monetary history of our civilization to lend support to this association. In the latter part of the nineteenth century and in the early twentieth century the "proper" stuff was gold. Earlier in the nineteenth century it was gold or silver or both. Gold and silver were the proper stuffs of the middle ages and during the early modern period.

During these periods other materials were also used: copper in the middle ages and later to adulterate silver; copper, brass, and nickel for petty coins. At various times in the last three centuries of western civilization monies have been made of paper, sometimes handwritten but mostly printed.* Sometimes the paper money "represented" a precious metal, as nineteenth-century copper and nickel coins were supposed to be immediately exchangeable into coins of the precious metal. At other times the paper money was "backed by" a productive asset or something which would generate an income of proper money stuff with which to redeem the paper money. Early in the eighteenth century John Law, working for the French monarchy, started a money "backed by" the productivity or value of the land of France's Mississippi Valley territory. British colonial governments in North America before the Revolution issued paper monies (bills of credit) "backed by" expected tax receipts. At other times the paper (or base metal) money was "backed by" nothing except the power of the state: it was legal tender. This kind of paper money is called "fiat" money (and base metal coins are called "token" money). At still other times the paper money was "backed" by nothing—unless one wants to say that the belief based on experience that people would accept the paper money is a "something."

There was some sense to saying that the paper or token "stood for" the "real" money when the Federal Reserve banknote on the Bank of England pound note promised to pay in gold, or when fifty token nickels could be exchanged for a $2.50 gold coin. There was in fact a great deal of sense in saying that the United States silver certificate was "backed by" silver since the United States government did buy and hold silver equal in value to the certificates (which were issued because people preferred to carry paper rather than coined silver dollars). There was less sense in saying that the pound note or the dollar bill promising payment in gold "stood for" or was "backed by" gold because, had holders of the notes and bills asked for the gold for which the paper "stood," many would have been disappointed: there just was not that much gold in Britain or in the United States.

Today—as in those times past when the paper money was "fiat"—the paper and the tokens "stand for" nothing except what they can do for their owners: make payments to payees who will accept the paper and tokens in payment. So far have we gone in dissociating money from any physical thing

---

*Paper money was produced centuries ago in East Asia. Marco Polo reported that the Chinese Emperor paid in a paper currency made of the inner bark of the mulberry tree, and insisted that it be accepted throughout his empire. These East Asian paper monies appear to have been acceptable because emperors and kings made them acceptable "or else."

that the largest quantity of money in the developed countries is in the form of "demand deposits" which "exist" only as a matter of "evidence in the records" but in no (other) physical form whatsoever. Some stuffs—dollar bills, pound notes, and the ledgers, bank statements, and magnetic tapes on which demand deposits are recorded—are best regarded as evidences of promises to pay or of the courts' commitment to forcing the creditor to accept payment in the banknotes of the nation's central bank. They have no utilitarian, aesthetic, or other treasurable value other than their use as evidence that a promise (by bank or government) exists. Paper monies have been so messed up with pictures and symbols and flecks that they are not, as paper, "worth the paper they're printed on." In these cases the stuff-in-itself is of no importance. What matters is that there is a record which can be used to enforce the rights and duties of members of the society. These stuffs are analogous to the records of land deeds in a county court house (and we do not say we have a "paper land" system).

# III

## TRADE, MONEY, AND MARKETS

In modern times trade, money, and markets have been so closely associated that we think of them as constituting, along with production, a single sphere of activities which we call "the economy." We transfer this perception of money in our economy to the Soviet Union, where it is true with modifications, and to the rest of the world, past and present, where it is often untrue.

### Money and Markets

In capitalist economies or national market economies the price paid for a good or service by customers, business firms, governments, or other organizations depends largely upon the processes of offering money (demand) for goods and services and of offering goods or services (supply) for money "on a market." The more money offered for a good or service, relative to the amounts offered for other goods or services, the larger will be the supply forthcoming because the larger amount of money will pay for the larger amount of resources (materials, machinery, labor, and so on) needed to produce the larger supply. The larger amount of money offered for a good encourages and allows the suppliers of the good to bid up the prices of goods and services used in producing that particular good and so to draw the productive inputs away from other uses, simultaneously increasing the supply of the good now in greater demand and reducing the supply of other goods. A change in one person's demand would not, of course, affect the operations of most modern businesses (although it would affect a bespoke tailor's efforts), but changes in the demands made by a number of people will affect the uses of inputs.

18

People's incomes depend largely on the prices they are offered for the productive inputs that they supply: labor, including skills, and the right to use the inputs, natural and man-made, in which they have property rights.

The markets on which the goods and services—both those used in production and those used by consumers, governments, and so on—are sold may be geographically limited or may be worldwide; there may be a few fixed physical centers or a large number of such centers; and a network of communications facilities may serve as the market. Markets for fresh milk have limited geographical scope, as do real-estate markets, while the market for coffee beans is worldwide. Contracts for future delivery of grain in the United States are mostly bought and sold in the Chicago Board of Trade building. For the world the center for buying and selling contracts for the delivery of metals is in London. The market for the various national monies (the foreign-exchange market) exists as a network of telephone and teletype lines connecting large centers around the world. Retail markets for food and clothing are spread over thousands upon thousands of stores. The markets which exist in different places—different food stores in a town, cotton markets in New Orleans, New York, and Bombay—are connected by the fact that demanders can buy in different places. A New Yorker can hardly buy his meat and potatoes in Chicago, but block by block, shopping center by shopping center, there are overlaps connecting New York and Chicago. A Hong Kong textile firm has the choice of buying cotton in Cairo, in New Orleans, or in São Paulo, Brazil. And the markets for different sorts of things are connected by the fact that demanders can substitute one thing for another: when the price of steak rises people can buy hot dogs instead, lentils substitute for meat, and evenings of bowling for a TV set. Businesses can substitute cash registers for people who can add, and oil for coal (or vice versa) in powering machinery.

Attracting inputs into different uses by offering money for their use has been called "capitalism," "the market system," the "self-regulating market system," the "free market system" and the "free-enterprise system" or "competitive system." It has not been the typical system of organizing the production and distribution of goods and services through human history; and today, insofar as economies are socialized, it is not dominant in decisions about what to produce and who shall get the output. In the communist countries the basic pattern of output is decided upon by the government. In other countries—Britain and India, for instance—many decisions are administrative or political—nonmarket decisions—and others are largely based on market prices. In the United States economy a great many decisions do not depend exclusively, or even primarily, on prices arrived at between those who offer money for goods and those who offer to supply the goods. The decision to land astronauts on the moon was a political decision made without anything like certain knowledge of the costs. How much money elderly people have to spend depends in good part upon decisions made by Congress-and-President in passing acts about social-security benefits. Equally political is the decision about how much dental care the dependents of members of the armed services will enjoy.

Nonmarket decisions are not made entirély independently of money measurements of costs. Had most advisors estimated the cost of landing on the moon at $200 billion the United States government would probably have decided against trying to land on the moon by 1970; and it would certainly have refused to try at a price tag of $500 billion.

By and large in private-enterprise economies the demand in money for one kind of good or another determines which goods will be produced and therefore how natural and human resources will be used, and which kinds of industry will expand capacity. Although this determination by private choice of consumers and the matching actions of business firms is modified by the effects of government taxing and spending, a rough rule of thumb is that three-fourths of decisions are made by private persons or private business firms.

What one finds throughout the world today is the use of money to pay out incomes in all cities and in the countryside of the developed countries; to keep accounts of all productive and distributive activities in the developed countries, whether capitalist, socialist, or communist; to keep accounts of all such activities in the underdeveloped countries where these activities are organized in modern institutions and in many activities which have not yet been brought completely within the orbit of modern institutions.

The now universal use of money in payment for all goods and services that are produced or supplied by the modernized sector of the world economy, the now widespread use of money in payment for many other goods and services, and the unity of markets in the nonsocialist world economy in the past century and a half—all are reasons why we think of money-production-trade-markets-economy as aspects of one unified system of human activity. Money is intimately associated with markets: incomes come from selling the power to use or direct the use of our resources (property) and labor, and the incomes paid in money determine how much of the world's wherewithal each of us gets to use. The way in which we get to use—acquire control over—goods and services is the payment of money in *exchange*. And the meanings or uses of *exchange* and *trade* have come to overlap very much: "He's in foreign trade," "He's a trader in metals," "The retail trade has been revolutionized by the supermarket," "Cincinnati was a center of trade in the middle west," are all statements about exchanges for money.

## Money and Markets in the Soviet Union

The uses of money in the Soviet Union[1] appear to correspond with their uses in free-enterprise and semisocialist economies. People get their purchasing power (command over goods and services) from wages and salaries. Consumer goods are distributed among families as they buy them in the stores with money. The state-owned industrial, commercial, and service enterprises receive money from the sale of their products to other firms and to families, and loans from the Soviet banks provide money to pay for expansion of their productive facilities.

There are, however, differences between the Soviet monetary system and the systems with which we are familiar. First, purchasing power does not determine what is done. Rather, decisions about what is to be done—where and how to develop which industries; among what goods and services the consumer will be allowed to choose—are made by the Communist Party and the planning agencies of the state. Prices are then set to help assure that the actions of people and the decisions of managers will correspond with or support the achievement of the Plan's objectives. Planners and managers at the levels of region and industry are asked to maximize profits, but asked to do so in the light of a set of prices which, for instance, encourages them to use lots of electrical power and heavy machinery, and to do so subject to planning decisions about the kind of product, wages, working conditions, and any other constraints the planners put upon the managers. In the 1930's (and since to a lesser degree) prices of agricultural produce were set low, the wages of industrial labor high to encourage the movement of people from farm to city. Consumers are allowed to choose the things they want to buy with the money they earn, but if there is a relatively high demand for one kind of good, that does not mean that more of that good is produced. High money demand for a good in short supply is sopped up by levying a "turnover tax," rather like a "wholesale sales tax," thus raising the price of the good, with much of the high price going to the state and not to the industry producing the good.

It is not that the state is not strong enough to direct people into the jobs the planners prefer them to enter, or strong enough to force managers to run industries with some conformity to the plans. Rather, it is that the use of money as an inducement means that the state need exert less force in achieving its aims. Also, the use of money provides ways of checking upon and evaluating performance. With prices set to reflect the aims and priorities of the planners, the examination of the profitability of plants can help reveal

---

[1]For sympathetic accounts of the Soviet economy see Maurice Dobb, *Soviet Economic Development Since 1917*, or Howard J. Sherman, *The Soviet Economy*. For less sympathetic accounts see Naum Jasny, *The Soviet Economy During the Plan Era*, or Nicolas Spulber, *The Soviet Economy: Structure, Principles, Problems*.

how successfully the plant managers are carrying out the objectives of the Plan (and, if it is felt desirable, other, nonpecuniary chops can be brought to bear on managers who are not doing what is wanted). Payments are made by plants and other enterprises to each other by transfers through the State Bank, thus making it possible for the Bank to monitor the progress and performance of each enterprise.

Another peculiarity of the Soviet system is that bank deposits are not interchangeable with paper money and coins. People but not enterprises use paper money and coins; and people do not use checking accounts.* Wages and salaries are paid in currency, not by check, and enterprises can get currency from the State Bank only to pay employees. This system is designed to make sure that the managers of enterprises do not get hold of money—a hard-to-trace kind of money—that they could use in ways other than those authorized by the plans. To minimize the possibility of unplanned use of currency by enterprises, stores receiving paper money and coins from their sales to people must immediately deposit the currency in the State Bank.†

The transfers of money from one enterprise to another through the State Bank are not checks, as we are used to checks, in that they are not transferable to third parties and can only be made for payments specifically authorized by the Plan. In this respect Soviet money, while exhibiting much of the appearance of a means of payment or medium of exchange, is largely a money of account, a means of public control, and not a source of economic power or a determinant of what things are done or how they are done. Although in form an enterprise makes payments with the money it receives from selling to other enterprises, in substance it has money at the Bank because the Plan authorizes it to have the money.

This is, of course, an idealized version. Reading about the Soviet economy will soon convince the reader that there are ways around Plans, and that when it becomes particularly difficult for a plant manager to fulfill his planned duties he can, somehow, get money to pay "expediters" to help him outside proper channels, or he can use the money flows to disguise changes in the goods or quality of goods his enterprise produces. Long lines in shops and feelings of frustration sometimes result from differences between what Russians as consumers want and what Soviet policy considers the best mix of products for the nation in the long run.

---

*People do have savings accounts, from which they can make payments to state enterprises instead of paying cash. However, these savings accounts are "cash substitutes," and are kept separate from all other bank accounts and transactions.

†There are "leakages" between the two parts of the system. The major one occurs because members of collective farms sell the produce of the small plots each is allowed for currency, so that it is impossible to separate their transactions as people from their transactions as producing enterprises.

The scheme of the Soviet economy and its use of money is certainly different from the systems in Britain, the United States, Germany, India, or Brazil. In these countries money-as-purchasing-power gives the possessor great power; in the Soviet Union power gives the possessor money-as-purchasing-power to carry out public policy in many aspects of life.

## Livelihood, Barter, and Money

The close association, verging on identity, of trade, money, and markets as different aspects of the same thing has not always characterized economies. There are today very few places indeed where there is no money, where people do not regard money as important. However, in the tribal and peasant societies of Africa and Asia, some or even most of the food people eat, the houses they live in, and the clothing they wear is not bought but produced and used within a small group, often a kin or village group, or by the members of peasant families. In medieval Europe little of the staple foodstuffs was sold in markets before the tenth and eleventh centuries, and even thereafter most of the food consumed in the countryside was consumed by the producing peasant families. In the ancient Near East the produce of farmers and artisans was contributed to the city temple and distributed from the temple to the members of the temple community, by rules of duty and of right rather than by sale and purchase. Even in the United States much of the food of small-farm families was supplied directly from their own produce well into the twentieth century. Only in the highly developed areas of the world is it the case that virtually all farm produce is sold and all food bought by farming families.

So used are we to buying things with the money we earn by working for wages and salaries, or by selling the right to use our property, that when asked what would happen if there were no money, we almost always strike immediately upon the idea of bartering one good or service for another. What we are doing in suggesting bartering as the alternative to our monetized market system has been called "speculative history" or "history by abstraction." It consists in taking our system as a whole, removing one element from the system, and then asking what we would do to provide a substitute for the missing element. Bartering or trading one item for another, without money as the intermediate medium of exchange, seems an obvious answer, since it reconstructs our system—our system of valuing, our operations of buying and selling, our institutions of property rights—with a minimum of alteration and hence of effort to understand. It "makes sense." The only trouble with the speculation is that it just isn't true, comparatively or historically. Whether we turn to the evidence from history or to the evidence in accounts by anthropologists, we do not find economic systems in which people depend upon bartering their labor or produce for the produce of others in order to get the necessities of daily life.

In any society of which we have accounts there has been division of labor, at the very least of roles between men and women, adults and children. The duties and privileges assigned by sex and age do not follow universal rules, as any reader of ethnographies will rapidly become aware, but in any society there are differentiations along these lines. In what we call more complex societies there are further divisions, some people being primarily farmers, others craftsmen or unskilled laborers or warriors or rulers. The variety of crafts and trades may be small or very large. Any society must have an economic system for reassigning the products from those who produce one sort of good or provide one sort of service to the others in that society. In our society we achieve this reassignment (economists call it the allocation of real income) by selling our product or the use of our property or labor and buying from others. It is said that the intermediation of money—in the formulation "Good for Money for Good"—eliminates the need for "double coincidence." Double coincidence expresses the idea that the producer of one good, who wants another good, must find a producer of the other good who wants the first producer's good. It is a logical formulation of the problem of integrating different productive activities, and has been illustrated in a dialogue:[2]

> "I have just made a fine pair of sandals. Will you give me some arrowheads for these sandals?"
> "We don't want any sandals. But if you have some bananas, we'll trade with you."
> "I don't have any bananas."
> "Sorry."

This represents "history by abstraction" at its crudest. Nowhere do people make sandals in a vague hope they will find others willing to barter. When people from a monetized society in which most goods are got by buying them with money find themselves in a situation without money, they "reinvent" money. In prisoner-of-war camps during World War II, cigarettes became a medium of exchange and a store of value. In this situation a money is found in order to reconstruct a system with which the participants are already familiar. But the fact that people who have used money find another money to use if they are deprived of the money they are used to does not mean that inventing a money with which to conduct trade is the "naturally human" way. Rather, the way humans naturally behave is to try to continue to use the systems they understand.

There are many systems which do not depend on trade or barter, at least not for the largest portion of the goods people consume. One system of organizing an economy with little trade but with a moderately extensive division of labor was that found in India's villages in the nineteenth century, a

---

[2]Ruth Below Grosse, *Money, Money, Money*, pp. 7-8.

system which survived in many areas into the twentieth century and of which remnants may be found in many villages within the last two decades.[3]

The peasantry of eighteenth- and nineteenth-century India lived in an economy in which coined money had been used for a long time, but production for sale was not the typical means of livelihood. Many payments were made in kind. The lowest orders in that society might never see a coin from one year to the next. There were peasants living close to towns who sold in the town markets, and with the spread of commercial opportunities some peasants became largely dependent upon the sale of their produce. This was true of the cotton farmers of Gujarat in western India during the nineteenth century and is the case with many sugar-cane farmers all over India in this century. The typical situation was, however, not that of a peasantry producing for sale in a market but of a peasantry tilling the land and dividing the crop with others in the village.

The Indian village was ruled by a "dominant" caste (sometimes it was the Brahmin or priestly caste, often one of the warrior castes, sometimes a lower, farming caste). Above the village in political organization were principalities or kingdoms or empires. The members of the dominant caste, through their headman, were responsible for paying a tribute (or tax, or land revenue, as the British called it) to the ruler. At some times and some places this payment was made in silver rupee coins, but often it was paid in kind, a share in the actual grain harvest.

Within the village one could distinguish several, even many levels in the hierarchies of power and prestige. Below the dominant caste were what might be called respectable cultivators who turned over a share of their harvests to the headman or the leading members of the dominant caste. The respectable farmers in turn had attached to themselves in inferior status laborers or permanent servants, who might on occasion change masters but who often served the same master as did their fathers and grandfathers. These people also shared in the harvest and often received daily handouts of food and whey. Cloth, woven by the women of the farmers' households, was also provided these servants.

---

[3]The literature on the Indian village is extensive. The nineteenth-century *Settlement Reports*, written by British officers about each district where they had assessed taxes on the land, give accounts of the rural economy of the area, often with much local economic history. (For an example of the use of these reports, see Walter C. Neale, *Economic Change in Rural India*, Chapter 3.) Since about 1950 there have been a large number of studies by anthropologists. Two dealing largely with the village economy as it existed in the 1950's are F. G. Bailey, *Caste and the Economic Frontier*, and T. Scarlett Epstein, *Economic Development and Social Change in South India*. The information on Epstein's villages is updated in her *South India: Yesterday, Today, and Tomorrow*. The literature on reciprocal rights and obligations within the village hierarchy is well surveyed, if with a Marxist bias, in Thomas O. Beidelman, *A Comparative Analysis of the Jajmani System*.

There were specialists in the village: blacksmiths, washermen, barbers, scribes, Brahmin priests. These specialists carried on their occupations as needed: repaired plows when they broke, washed the clothes or shaved the men of the families to which they were attached, kept the village records, officiated at ceremonies. Each of these persons took a share from the harvest of the cultivating families to which they were attached.

In this Indian village system the problem of double coincidence did not arise. Every needed person was there, his role and duties known to all. Each carried out his duties, providing a portion of the goods or services used by the villagers, and receiving an assortment of goods and services from others. There was no necessary role for money in this system. Each was assured his share because each carried out his duties and each had his understood, customary rights to a part of the whole.

To characterize the system as a "happy family" would be highly misleading. The members of the dominant caste got the lion's share of the village's output: a lion's share, however, of what was usually a meager output. The lowest orders did well to average a pound of grain per head a day and a few yards of rough cloth per year. There could be disagreements about whether the share one received was as much as one deserved. The argument, however, was not an argument over the "price" of the labor or the harrow but over whether in fact the customary payment had been made in full. (A right to ten double handfuls from a heap of grain does allow room for recriminations over how double and how full the hands were.) Arguments were muted, for violence could be and often was the recourse of the powerful in the village. One does not argue long and hard with a man who offers to have you beaten by his gang of toughs.

If dissatisfied, a person could flee the village, but fleeing involved dangers. Where would one be welcomed? Would one be killed while wandering in search of a new place? Up to the middle of the nineteenth century there was vacant land and new villages could be established. A small village might welcome a larger population for defense, to achieve fuller utilization of its land, to fill out its complement of village artisans and servants. So a better situation might be found, and this option did limit the exploitative tendencies of the powerful, but nowhere could one escape the power of the established.

The village was not totally self-sufficient. Iron and salt came from outside. The richer in the village might want some of the finer goods produced in the towns. Here often money was needed, but its use was peripheral to the daily round. Quantification is impossible from the records, but the descriptions do suggest that—in terms of modern prices or in terms of any other measure such as weight or volume—less than ten percent of what was used or consumed in the village was bought outside the village, and that a village could go on functioning normally for a year or more if it had to do so without some of the goods got from outside. (Today in rural India no bent nail goes unrecycled, so the only loss of iron is from rusting.) Furthermore, only a few people needed to engage in purchasing from outside. Once within the village, salt could be distributed through the normal network of dependence.

Money was, of course, useful. When the powerful lived in a village near a town or city they could sell their share of the crop and buy finer goods than those which wives, daughters-in-law, and village artisans could make. At the end of the sixteenth century the Mughal Emperor Akbar tried to change village tribute in kind into payments in money, but the historical record does not show how successful he was. As late as the last half of the nineteenth century in principalities that had been parts of Akbar's empire the tribute was still paid in kind. Mentions of moneylenders in villages date back centuries, but there is no evidence that moneylending was a common occupation throughout rural India, as distinguished from a profession limited to areas where the administrative and commercial towns had had an impact and to dealings only with those few who had opportunity to participate directly in the larger economy.

Rules about what jobs each person or family was to do and rules about how the products of the jobs were to be distributed among the members of the village provided a system which had no need for money or for barter.

Elsewhere other rules have assured that the product of divided labor will be distributed among all members of society. Malinowski's accounts of the Trobriand Islanders (who live northeast of New Guinea) provide a number of examples.[4] A man did not consume the yams he grew, the staple of the Trobriand diet, but gave them to his brother-in-law, the rule being that a man supported his mother, his sisters' families, or the family of his nearest female relative. Thus the network of kinship and marriage was the system for distributing the staple foodstuffs. In addition, chiefs were provided with large amounts of yams because they had a number of wives and therefore a number of brothers-in-law. The yams given to the chiefs were distributed by the chiefs at feasts, and the exhibition of the large amount of yams the chief stored in open-latticed huts evidenced his importance and superiority.

Other goods moved from person to person by gift. There was a wide range of variation in the kind, circumstance, and time and nature of countergift attached to any gift-giving. Malinowski distinguished seven classes of gift, from the "pure" gift, which mutually obligated and rewarded husband and wife, son and father, to "trade, pure and simple." When dealing with the people from interior villages who made dishes, combs, lime pots, armlets,

[4]For Bronislaw Malinowski's work, see the books cited in the References and Bibliography. There are two selections from Malinowski's work reprinted in Dalton, *Tribal and Peasant Economies:* "*Kula*: the Circulating Exchange of Valuables in the Archipelagoes of Eastern New Guinea," pp. 171-184; and "Tribal Economics in the Trobriands," pp. 185-223.

and baskets, the agriculturalists bartered in the way one thinks of barter happening: a haggling over the amount of goods to be handed over in exchange. Many "exchanges," however, involved long-term trading partners, and customary rates of recompense. After the harvest inland agriculturalists brought quantities of yams to partners in a fishing village. Later the fisherman sent word that they were going fishing and the agriculturalists came down and took the catch home to their own village. The fishing villagers used the yams in distributions at mortuary feasts; the agricultural villagers distributed fish at such feasts. So much fish was taken back to the agricultural village that large quantities spoiled before the proper recipient of the fish got delivery. Delivery of yams, by depositing them on front of the hut of the fishing partner," is an invitation, which *never* can be rejected, to return the gift by its *fixed equivalent* in fish."[5]

Similarly, long-distance trade was carried on with permanent partners. The ceremonial centerpiece of this trade was the Kula Ring, an arrangement among a number of Melanesian peoples whereby red shell necklaces traveled clockwise around a circuit of hundreds of miles involving peoples of a number of different cultures, while shell armbands traveled from trading partner to trading partner in the reverse direction. Each necklace and armband acquired a history as it circulated along the Ring, and with a history acquired greater and greater prestige and was considered somehow more valuable. Along with the ceremonial gift and countergift went goods of Trobriand manufacture, some for gift in expectation of countergift from the distant trading partner, some for barter with anyone who wanted the manufactures.

Barter was an element in the Trobriand economic system, but successful barter was not needed for access to gardens to grow the staple yams. Continuity of supply of various items not produced in a village was assured by the existence of permanent trading partners and mutually understood standards of proper recompense for the delivery of a good. Trobrianders did not need to worry about the occurrence of a "double coincidence"—they knew from whom and to whom they would receive and give what. It was a system without a money, with some barter, but mostly with other ways of distributing goods so that livelihood did not depend on trade.

## Trade and Money

No one can know the origins of money or the origins of trade. The origins are buried in the pasts of nonliterate societies. Our first record of coined money is that of the Lydian Greeks in Asia Minor in the seventh century B.C., but that is not necessarily the first use of items in one or another moneyish use.

---

[5]Bronislaw Malinowski, "Tribal Economics in the Trobriands," in Dalton, *Tribal and Peasant Economies*, p. 216. Italics mine.

There is no persuasive reason to believe that money and trade originated together, or that money originated in trade. We have in both the historical record and the accounts of anthropologists ample evidence of trade without money, and also of the moneyish uses of things without money being used in trade. It has been suggested that money emerged first and separately as a means of *noncommercial* payment:[6] cattle and pigs and shells in marriage and in fines; shells and pigs and cloths in payment of initiations and promotions in cults and societies. Perhaps separately it emerged as a way of keeping palace, temple, and imperial accounts: in ancient Mesopotamia the accounts of the city temples were expressed in silver, although payment seems largely to have been made in barley and oil. In Oceania pigs are used in payment, but mostly in payment of fines and for entrance and promotion in secret societies.

One finds in the archaeological record items which must have been produced one place and then moved to another place hundreds, even thousands of miles distant. This evidence is often taken as proof of trade between the places, or trade via intermediaries. In many cases it may reflect such trade, but things can move other than by trade: when things from elsewhere are wanted, they can be gathered by traveling to the place where the things are, picking them up, and bringing them home. Where there are people in possession of things, the travelers-in-search can take the things by violence or threat thereof: cattle raiding in Africa and Scotland; Dutch management of the spice trade with the Indies; Spanish looting among the Aztecs and Incas. How Catholic chalices got into ninth- and tenth-century Norse homes is explained by the great Christian prayer of the time: "Lord preserve us from the fury of the Vikings." One anthropologist has suggested that trade in the Solomon Islands may have begun with "the raping of women and children."[7] When the people in possession are strong enough to resist, or able to run away with the things, there we find a two-way movement of goods, or payment. The root of the difference between seizure and trade is clearly illustrated by the contrast between the behavior of the Dutch in the Indies on the one hand and their behavior trading with the powerful empires and kingdoms in China and India.

When there is trade between two peoples something moneyish may emerge as a means of payment and is apt to emerge as a standard of value or unit of account. Cowries, gold dust, and slaves became the money of west African trade with the Europeans in the sixteenth through eighteenth centuries. Accounts in the North American Indian trade were kept in furs, and in the early days payment was made in the strings of shells called wampum. But a money need neither be struck upon or consciously invented. In the Congo,

---

[6]A. Hingston Quiggin, *A Survey of Primitive Money: The Beginning of Currency*, p. 322.

[7]Richard C. Thurnwald, "Pigs and Currency in Buin: Observations About Primitive Standards of Value and Economics," in Dalton, *Tribal and Peasant Economies*, p. 241.

pygmies exchanged with the full-sized people in "silent trade." In "silent trade" a group (A) leaves goods for the other group (B) and disappears. Group B comes, gathers up the goods, and leaves goods of its own in exchange. Group A returns and, if satisfied with what was left, takes it. If not satisfied, Group A departs without taking the goods left and Group B comes back and adds to the pile: no standards of value, no means of payment other than the goods of trade themselves.

The Phoenicians were *the* traders of the ancient world, yet they did not use a money. They traded in precious metals but did not use coins even after others had started to do so.

Trade has often been official or royal, carried on as an aspect of foreign affairs. Solomon received cedars and gold from Hiram of Tyre; he supplied Hiram with labor and with twenty cities. It was not silent trade, for when Hiram saw the cities "and they pleased him not, he said, What cities are these which thou has given me, my brother? And he called them the land of Cabul"—a remark some think showed that Hiram did not regard those twenty cities as suitable recompense. Nevertheless Hiram sent another six score talents of gold.[8] This was not commercial trade, but gift and countergift in a political alliance. The Egyptian Pharaohs traded abroad when they had to, but when they "traded" with the area to the south or with the Sinai peninsula they sent their soldiers to take or to mine.[9] A David or a Solomon could bring the Pharaohs to trade rather decently, in gift and countergift, including a daughter of Pharaoh for Solomon, but when the Israelites were weak Pharaoh took what he wanted from them.

Money then, and despite our own close intermeshing of the three ideas, is to be differentiated from markets and trade. There can be money with little in the way of markets, and certainly without money demand dominating the markets and the markets in turn dominating man's uses of nature, himself, and his tools. There can be trade without money and there can be trade without markets.

---

[8]I Kings 9:12-14, *Holy Bible*, American Standard Version.

[9]For an account of the ancient Egyptian economic system see Henri Frankfort, *The Birth of Civilization in the Near East*, pp. 90-120.

# IV

## WHO, WHAT, WHEN, AND HOW:
## MONEY USES ILLUSTRATED

What have been called monies by one person or another has depended very much on what traits, characteristics, or uses each person has thought essential to the idea of money. For instance, some have regarded cattle among the pastoral and semipastoral peoples of Africa as money,[1] yet Evans-Pritchard, whose account of the Nuer of the southern Sudan was one of the formative studies of what are sometimes called "cattle cultures," states flatly that the Nuer had no money.[2] The more the number of traits, characteristics, and uses discussed in Chapter I which a person feels is needed for something to be a money, the fewer will be the number of societies which could be said to have a money. This chapter deals with monies in several tribal societies. The monies are borderline cases: some people would feel that these are not properly monies, others that they do fall within an acceptable definition of money. They are dealt with here because they illustrate the variety of ways in which moneyish stuffs are integrated with different systems of social organization and perform differing functions in different societies.

No money can be used to fulfill any and all obligations in any society, or to

---

[1]Harold K. Schneider, *The Wahi Wanyaturu: Economics in an African Society*, and Peter Rigby, *Cattle and Kinship Among the Gogo: A Semi-Pastoral Society of Central Tanzania*, treat Wanyaturu and Gogo cattle very much as money. In my discussions in the late 1950's with Conrad Arensberg (Anthropology, Columbia University) and Paul Bohannan (Anthropology, Northwestern University) both felt that where cattle were used in several kinds of payments one should classify the cattle as money.

[2]E. E. Evans-Pritchard, *The Nuer*, p. 88.

acquire any and every sort of good or performance. At the other extreme, no one calls an item or process money if it cannot be used to fulfill at least two kinds of obligation or to measure at least two kinds of otherwise disparate things or actions. But between these extremes one can differentiate among those monies which have many uses and those which have fewer, even few indeed. The monies so differentiated cannot, however, be laid along a continuum with, for instance, modern money at one end and African cattle at the other, for there are ways in which some special-purpose monies are used but in which multipurpose money is not.

Monies vary greatly in respect to *what* can be paid for or measured by a money; *who* can (or must) make the payments: *when* (in what circumstances) the payments are made or the values measured; and *how* (in what forms, with what procedures) the payments are made or the values measured.

What things or services are for sale varies from society to society. In some, one can buy land; in others, land cannot be sold. In the United States, privately owned land can be sold easily, but public land is now rarely for sale. At some times and places people can be sold; other societies prohibit slavery. Until recently in many western countries women could not buy and sell land; and it has been common in western societies to forbid women to engage in any except petty monetary transactions. Today if a seven-year-old offers a store a $20 bill to spend on bubblegum the shopkeeper is very apt to telephone a parent and ask if she knows that little Willy has a $20 bill: seven-year-olds are allowed to pay with pennies but not with twenties. Some transactions require immediate payment. In others a period is allowed before payment. Some payments in our society must be made in currency; others can be made by check or by credit card; and still others by signing an IOU of one sort or another. Sometimes and in some places an obligation to pay is expressed in money terms but the actual payments are made in unmoneyish things.

In describing and analyzing the roles of monies in different societies, one is dependent upon the accounts given by the scholars who have studied each society. For literate societies, one can go to the original records and documents oneself, but except in his own line of research a historian depends on the work of other historians. For nonliterate societies, the source must be the reports of the anthropologists who have lived in them. As is true of every profession, there are disagreements over what are the best methods of research, presentation, and interpretation. Some anthropologists have tried to reconstruct how a society was organized before it was much influenced by colonial governments or other contacts with European nations. Some describe societies which are undergoing continuous change and adaptation to new situations. Some depend more than others on questioning respondents; others prefer to rely more on their eyes. The reports of anthropologists are influenced by the particular aspects of social organization or culture in which each is especially interested. The reports are also influenced by the training, beliefs, and theoretical approach of each anthropologist. The first account below is of the Lele. Perhaps it might better be called an account of Mary Douglas's Lele. It has even been said that one should think of the source as the Lele's Mary Douglas, and so on for each report—the Kapauku's Pospisil, the Buin's Thurnwald—because the account we have of the society is a three-component product of the anthropologist and the people studied and the effects of the experience on the anthropologist. (The same could be said about any scholar's work in any subject.) The ethics of scholarship have kept the reports honest, and having no other source one accepts the ethnographies as written, with the knowledge that the ethnographies are not the peoples themselves but another human being's report on them. It has been said, for instance, that the picture of Kapauku society presented by Leopold Pospisil seems at variance with the pictures of other New Guinea tribes as reported by others. In this chapter I have chosen to present the information, as best I can, as it has been presented by the anthropologists who have studied each people. When the anthropologist has used the "anthropological" (or abstract) present, I have done so.

## Raffia Cloth among the Lele

The Lele,[3] a small tribe of the Kasai region of what was the Belgian Congo and is now Zaire, produce a cloth made of the combed fibers of a kind of palm. Well-combed and closely woven, the cloth is regarded by other tribes of the area as of superior quality. Two lengths, sewn together, make the skirt which constitutes the Lele's garb. All Lele males, young and old, can weave the cloth, as much as five lengths in a day, although that is considered very strenuous work. As clothing the raffia skirt will last about four months, but it is not as a garment but as a treasured item, a store of value, and a means of payment and of "foreign" trade that the raffia cloth is most important for the Lele.

In "foreign trade"—that is, in trade with the neighboring tribesmen for calabashes, arrowheads, hoes, knives, bells, other iron work, pottery, fish, baskets, camwood, and game—the Lele pay in raffia cloth. It is the means of payment preferred by the payees. The Cokwe, who take the cloth in payment for game, do not wear it but use it again in their other "foreign" trade. For the Cokwe it thus appears to be a "medium of foreign exchange," but for the other tribes it appears to be a desired commodity of import for use.

Within the Lele community the cloth is a means of payment, but not primarily of commercial payment. It is given to fathers when the son reaches

---

[3]A fuller description of the Lele economy is to be found in Mary Douglas, "Raffia Cloth Distribution in the Lele Economy," and in her "The Lele—Resistance to Change," pp. 183-213 in Paul Bohannan and George Dalton, editors, *Markets in Africa*. Page numbers in the text refer to "Raffia Cloth Distribution" in Dalton, *Tribal and Peasant Economies*.

adulthood, to wives when they bear children, to wives when they report "a would-be seducer," to fathers-in-law and mothers-in-law upon marriage, to the cult groups when one is admitted to membership, and to those who perform healing rites or divinations. A man also buries 20 of his cloths with a deceased father- or mother-in-law. Compensation for adultery is paid in cloth, as are fines for fighting in the village.

Raffia cloths are a means of payment and a medium of exchange, analogous to our money, when a carved drum or bellows or cup is bought from a skilled craftsman who is not a close relative. But when taking baskets, fishtraps, looms, dishes, and fur hats from kinsmen, the one or two cloths given in "recognition" of the relationship are clearly not "payment for value" as that is measured in trade with foreigners or in purchases from unrelated skilled artisans.

Lele males could produce much more raffia cloth than they do. Rather than spend twenty days producing 100 cloths for a bridewealth payment—the payment made by a groom's kin to the kin of the bride—or another 100 cloths which were owed as a fine for a discovered adultery, the men in one family borrowed from maternal and paternal relatives; sold meat; substituted francs (at the rate of 10 Belgian francs to one cloth), a she-goat, and camwood bars; and postponed full payment. To borrow from others is proof that one is admired, is of good credit, possesses dignity; and these virtues would not be established by weaving one's own cloth.

A collective bridewealth payment involves similar features. There are village wives assigned to an age set of younger men who do not yet have their own wives and the village as a whole is parent to the offspring of these wives. When one of its collective sons marries, the village is responsible for paying the bridewealth, but the obligation may be carried as a debt for as long as twenty years. This bridewealth debt is not paid with cloths the villagers have woven for the purpose but rather with cloths owed to the village when it has received them in repayment of loans made earlier by the village.

Raffia cloth is important in Leleland, as many other moneyish items are elsewhere, for the validation of control over women or for payment of dues that give one status or dignity. For the older men, who can weave relatively more efficiently than they can farm, and who have already acquired cloth by marrying off daughters, by reason of being insulted or cuckolded, and by receiving a share in the cloths paid by new members of the cult groups, the "raffia system" provides a form of old-age pension: younger men who need cloths must treat the elders moderately decently, even if resentfully. Wives, fifteen years and more younger than the husband, are there, paid for in the past, to feed and care for the older men.

Most of the everyday needs of each Lele are provided by the working units of self, family, age-mates, and relatives who share jointly in work and product. Houses—the huts of palm ribs and leaves and thatch—are not bought or rented. Most food, other than some game and fish, is not bought. What is needed for physical survival as well as most items of utility are provided without trade or purchase by the family, kin, and age-set groups.

If a Lele does not have and cannot or will not produce a desired item, he asks a kinsman for it, and if the kinsman does not have it or refuses to give it, the seeker will do without rather than buy it with raffia. Douglas could not buy raffia from the Lele, and got her raffia only by buying from the Belgian tribunal to which the Lele paid fines and taxes in raffia ("and even there the native clerks were reluctant to sell large quantities"—p. 114).

Among the Lele (as among the cattle cultures of Africa, the Kapauku, the Buin, and the New Hebrideans—all discussed later in this chapter), there is credit and debt, much lending and borrowing.

Ideas of credit do not come after the development of technological sophistication but may exist in complex and long-term forms in societies which are nonliterate and backward in the crafts and arts of agriculture, construction, and manufacturing.

Among the Lele, as among the other societies described later in this chapter, their money would buy things and performances which western monies cannot buy in western societies. I have yet to hear of a wife being given $20 for reporting a would-be seducer. (I trust that the growth of women's liberation will prevent the spread of this culture trait to our society.) Who could use raffia money was not restricted, but what it could be used for was—it was not used to buy food, except meat from foreigners, nor to buy houses nor to buy or rent land. It could be used, as Douglas discovered, to buy what she wanted from the Lele, but among the Lele it was not usually so used.* The answer to the question "When was it used?" is "largely, but not exclusively, on occasions of ritual or ceremony, and in compensation of wrongdoing." Raffia also served very often as a standard of value for payments which were made either in promises of raffia payment in the future or in substitutes such as Belgian francs and bars of camwood.

---

*In any account of the uses of money in a society one should be wary of one possibility: that the members of the society allow foreigners to use money in ways in which they would not allow each other to use it. This can occur either as a courtesy to the foreigner (an American in India or Britain is immediately forgiven actions which would earn opprobrium if done by an Indian in India or by an Englishman in Britain) or because some arrangement must be created or allowed to permit dealings between the members of society and the foreigners who do not have access to the normal modes of social intercourse: Douglas did not weave, nor did her husband, and neither she nor he had close kin among the Lele. The same considerations apply in evaluating reports of traders and administrators.

## Shells and Markets, Pigs and Politics

The Kapauku[4] of the mountains of New Guinea, who utilize a stone-age technology, have a highly monetized system for the distribution of goods and for the acquisition of personal prestige and political power. The goods produced or imported, both food and artifacts, are bought and sold for payment in shells, of which there is a variety of types in rather stable exchange relationship with each other. Land can be bought or rented by paying shells. Labor can be hired for payment in shells. Shells are the medium of exchange; they are the standard of deferred payment for the debts which organize the Kapauku society politically. They are a store of value, a man sometimes pledging not to use some of his shells at all but to pass them on to his heirs.

Shells will buy tobacco and pork; they will buy stone axes imported from the north; they will buy steel axes and machetes imported from the south coast. They will "pay for" wives, who cannot be had without payment. A boy once grown must pay his foster father for "services rendered." To form a "best-friendship" requires payment in shells, and expressions of sympathy at a death by distant relatives or strangers must be recompensed with a shell payment. "Almost all crimes can be settled through a proper transfer of shell currency" (p. 22). In contrast to our society, most sales take place between closely related members of the local kin group. From the ages of ten or eleven a person can have his own shell money and lend it even to his father, who thus becomes obligated to his son. A man without shells is a "tramp" (p. 18).

The Kapauku delight in speculation: they take pride in having bought very cheaply or sold very dearly; they buy bailer shells, an item of uncertain supply from the coast, when the bailer shells are in large supply and cheap, hoard them in caches in the cliffs, and sell when the bailers become scarce and dear.

Wealth is the main objective of life for Kapauku men and the Kapauku define wealth quite specifically in shells, in pigs, and in debts. A wealthy man has more land, more wives, and more shells, pigs, and debtors than other men; but he does not dress differently nor house himself differently nor use different tools from theirs. The wealthy eat well, the poor eat badly; but otherwise the material standard of living of rich and poor is much the same. What the wealthy man can have is political leadership in conciliating and solving disputes within his sublineage or lineage, in representing his sublineage or lineage to allied lineages, and—if he rises to the top of a confederacy—in dealing in foreign relations with other confederacies and leading his confederacy in war. Wealth alone will not make a man a leader, a *tonowi*—for he must also be generous.

Wealth is acquired by the successful breeding and sale of pigs and their

---

[4]The reader will find an account of Kapauku society and economy in Leopold J. Pospisil, *The Kapauku Papuans of West New Guinea*. Page numbers in the text refer to this book.

meat. One starts with a bit of a garden and a pig from his father, or a pig borrowed from someone else. Piglets lead to pigs, and pigs to sows, and sows to piglets, and so on to sales or loans of pork and pigs. Pigs must be fed, and that requires sweet potatoes. Sweet potatoes must be grown, and that requires wives—to weed the plots and harvest the potatoes; to feed cooked, chewed potatoes to the piglets; and to teach the piglets to grub (thus attaching the piglet to the man's wife, not to the piglet's mother). Therefore, more wives, more pigs. However, wives must be serviced and cannot be kept if dissatisfied, so the record number of eleven wives appears the limit to this form of pig dealing. Marriage as the road to wealth having been exhausted, one lends piglets, the borrower getting some pork when the pig is slaughtered, or a piglet or 20 kawane (the least valuable shell) if she is a sow who gives birth.

The wealthy man is admired. But he had also better be generous, for otherwise he is held in contempt. If he is generous he has followers: each "gift" is a loan which must be repaid. Those who have borrowed do not want to repay, for they are using the loans to amass wealth, yet the lender can call in his loan. The lender's heir not only can call in the loan; he is only too likely to do so. The debtor wants to keep the lender both happy and alive and so provides the lender with political support. The man with pigs and land also feeds "apprentices" who may expect the loan of pigs and cowries to pay for a bride when that time comes and who meanwhile serve both as bodyguards and as rather lazy laborers.

Borrow, breed, get; breed, marry, breed; sell, buy, breed; sell, marry, lend, and amass pigs and debtors and bodiga (the most valuable shell).

Anyone aged ten years or more of either sex can have shells and lend them and so indebt others who will not want to repay. But only men engage in the wheeler-dealer business of owning and lending pigs and amassing great wealth.

The processes and consequences of this monetized system differ in some respects from our own. The possession and use of wealth gains prestige, leadership, and security of food and physical safety. It does not, however, lead to the acquisition of an increasing variety of goods and services for one's private use. There are no "big houses on the hill," no lawns, no tennis-club memberships, no trips to Monte Carlo, or no collections of seventeen tweed sports coats. When necklaces of money shells and beads are bought they are often lent to others to wear.

While land can be bought, if the price paid is not the proper and traditional price the seller can demand the land back upon tendering the less-than-proper amount received. If the seller does not ask for the land back in these circumstances, his heirs are free to do so. An old man cannot sell his land without his sons' permission, and if he does so the sons can tender the purchase price and retrieve the land. Clearly one can buy land in Kapaukuland, but equally clearly buying land in Kapaukuland is not the same transaction, not done according to the same rules and not done with the same consequences, as buying land in the United States.

Purchases of sows are complex affairs: a down payment followed by a further payment when the sow and some of her offspring are killed, and a final payment of one or more female piglets. But if the sow dies early, then the deal is off and her carcass can be returned and the down payment demanded back. So too can the transaction be abrogated if the sow proves sterile. Here the Kapauku reverse our rule of the market place: theirs is "Let the seller beware."

Dealings in pigs are closely associated with feasts. A *juwo* feast is announced by the sponsor and his younger cosponsors months in advance. A dance house with a springy floor is built and for months before the feast people come from all about to dance up and down on the floor, to sing, and to flirt. A solo singer can mourn a death, ask for a loan, threaten a legal suit, or make proposals marital or indecent to a girl. At these events the Kapauku learn "the news and problems of the village. They also discover important relationships between individuals that otherwise would remain undetected. . . . it is as though one were dancing, singing, listening to new poetry, witnessing disputes and matchmaking, reading the newspaper, and participating in a cocktail party—all at the same time" (p. 75). On the day of the feast as many as 2,000 people gather to buy pork, to sell pigs, and to buy and sell all other wares. Loans are repaid and new loans contracted. Alliances are discussed and wars planned. The sponsor and cosponsors make a large profit on the sales.

To sponsor a feast one must be a rich and important man. He must help marshal the labor to build the dance house. At various times in the proceedings, and to various relatives, there must be gifts of pork. Lesser men do not, and presumably cannot, announce that they are giving a feast.

There is another kind of feast, also announced months in advance, whose purpose is to allow the sponsors to raise shells for blood money or some other purpose. The gatherings to dance and sing in the months leading up to this kind of feast are not so elaborate (there is no dance hall) nor so revealing of news. The focus is the donation, or properly the lending or advancing, of shells to the sponsors. There is also a good deal of buying and selling of pigs and wares.

In addition to feasts, there is an informal gathering for the "mass exchange of goods," which likewise is announced by a sponsor.

It appears that the transfer of goods among the Kapauku is significantly concentrated at these feasts, rather than, as in our society, occurring continuously and fairly evenly from day to day. Also, the transfer of goods seems to be closely associated not only with the prestige of the sponsor, his power and his pelf, but also with the organizing and continuance of social and political life. If the feasts combine the functions of Wall Street, the New Orleans cotton futures market, and the slaughterhouses of Chicago, they do so in a setting one might liken to a United States Federal District Court sitting in the House of Representatives.

*Who* among the Kapauku can use shell money for *what*? *When* and *how* do they use it? Just about anyone can use money for paying for just about anything whenever he wants anything, or whenever he wants someone else to do or not to do something. He can pay by handing over the appropriate denominations of their shell money *or* he can promise to do so in the future. It should be noted that credit and debt, on varying terms and for varying periods, are integral elements of the Kapauku system. Compared to western society, Kapauku society permits a wider range of money uses than do we. Since nearly any action can have a price, the Kapauku cannot have that gray moral area of money transactions that we call corruption. Money transactions permeate family relationships far more than they do in western society. Westerners may deal within the family in money—allowances to children, or food money for wives—but suits by ten-year-olds against fathers for unpaid debts do not occur. But money uses in Kapaukuland are not our money uses plus, without a minus. Land sales are restricted in respect of price, if the sale is to be binding, and an elderly man with grown sons cannot sell land for money without permission.

## Another Place, Other Pigs

The Buin of the Solomon Islands[5] used shells and pigs in ways similar to the ways in which the Kapauku use them. Among the Buin, women, pigs, and shells were the center of interest. Shells, on strings as long as from a man's chest to his outstretched hand, were lent or advanced and repaid. Feasts on pigs and pudding were the major events of Buin life. Bridewealth and bloodwealth were paid in strings of shells. Pots, bags, baskets, knives, arrows, spears, bows, feathers, and arm rings were bought for shells. Shells and pigs were exchanged between the families of husband and wife at a birth and at various rites as the child grew up. Shells were also used to pay for magical devices and incantations for help in garden work, or to seal a political alliance.

There were differences from the Kapauku system. Whereas in Kapauku-land any kind of food was buyable and sellable and often bought and sold, in Buin (in the days before European rule had much effect) women would not buy taro, the staple of the diet. Families were self-sufficient for the necessities of livelihood, and "a lazy or inefficient couple [was] fed by their kinsfolk" (p. 238). It appears that only in Kapaukuland would a man and his family suffer malnutrition because he lacked land and the wherewithal in

---

[5]This account is taken from Richard C. Thurnwald, "Pigs and Currency in Buin." Page numbers in the text refer to Dalton, *Tribal and Peasant Economies*.

shells to buy or rent land. Elsewhere in Oceania he would lack respect but not a decent supply of food.[6]

There was a hereditary Buin aristocracy which laid claim to all the land. The lower orders of society (the *kitere*), who could be described as bondsmen, could sell land only with the consent of the lord, and shared the proceeds with the lord. Since the aristocrat claimed all the land in his district, the right of the *kitere* to sell land with consent appears to have been restricted to sales within the aristocrat's domain. The *kitere* could not sell a pig, nor slaughter and eat one, without the consent of the lord. But when, with consent, the *kitere* sold his pig or presented it to his lord, he was paid for it.

Among the Buin, shell money and pigs fitted into a hierarchical society in which ancestry rather than wealth was the primary basis of power. Among the Buin the display of wealth and the giving away of pork at feasts was the proof of chieftainry, and Thurnwald emphasizes good will rather than debt as the important consequence of feasts. Surplus payments over and above an agreed price were made, and *kitere* made excess payments to their lords to assure good will.*

The who-what-when-and-how of money uses among the Buin presents contrasts with as well as similarities to money uses in western societies. Dealing in shells-for-pigs and pigs-for-shells would buy kinds of power and prestige which no rich man in western societies can buy with money. Among the Buin, birth into the aristocracy gave one opportunities for swine-wealth which has no counterpart among the children of United States congressmen. No one in Buin would have said "violence will get you nowhere"—they all

---

[6]Paul Einzig, *Primitive Money: In Its Ethnological, Historical, and Economic Aspects*, 2nd edition, pp. 47-50.

*As the reader of ethnographies will be aware, there is always a problem in deciding whether accounts of two peoples by different anthropologists reflect differences in the peoples and their ways or differences in the anthropologists' perceptions of the peoples. For instance, Pospisil seems, to this reader, to have a propensity to regard all interpersonal dealings in respect of material goods as reflections of that aspect of human character which has created the secondhand-car market. He also seems to feel that it reflects well on the Kapauku that some pretty awful brutality is directed toward past behavior and not designed to interfere with an individual's future freedom of action: "parents never use punishment to force a child into a certain behavior. Rather, it is a reprimand for past bad behavior" (Pospisil, *The Kapauku Papuans of West New Guinea*, p. 91). Similarly, Pospisil explains that the Kapauku would never imprison a person: no torture, they just shoot an arrow into an offender's leg (*ibid.*, pp. 42, 48). Pospisil does say that the offender is free to run away rather than be shot, but he does not say what alternative chop awaits the runaway. Conversely, Thurnwald says "that wealth requires the participation of the kinsmen and community to be enjoyed; . . . that wealth is . . . a socializing force . . . in spreading goodwill . . . and in supporting social solidarity" ("Pigs and Currency," p. 236 in Dalton, *Tribal and Peasant Economies*) but does not make clear what chop, if any, might await a *kitere* who did not make "excess" payments. Thurnwald, however, makes no effort to explain away the brutality of warfare, terrorism, and rape among the Buin.

knew it would get you women and pigs and shells. On the other hand, *kitere* were not allowed to deal freely in buying and selling with shell money. The Buin as well as the Kapauku systems also contrast with our system in that in those systems one must be swine-rich to be a leader: there was no rising through union or party or bureaucratic ranks to positions of great power and prestige while remaining at least "not rich."

## Cattle as Money

Cattle are often used in moneyish ways in Africa, especially in east Africa. The major money-like uses of cattle reported in earlier days were: the payment of cattle by the groom's kin group to the bride's; the payment of cattle in compensation (settlement) of a bloodfeud; the payment and repayment of cattle for cattle in a system of mutual friendship, alliance, and dependence; and the counting of cattle in evaluating the wealth of a man or a lineage. Cattle were often also used in payment of fines (compensation) to an offended party, a frequent reference being to fines for adultery, paid by a man to the man with whose wife he had slept. More recently, with the expansion of markets in the twentieth century, cattle have been used in payments of a commercial nature.

Each of the societies in which cattle play a primary role differs in various respects from the others. Each has experienced changes since the mid-nineteenth century resulting from contacts with colonial and more recently national governments and from contacts with the organizations and markets of the world economy. Some, like the Masai, are almost entirely herding societies. Other societies combine herding with agriculture. In the latter cases, although measurement might show that the societies derived more real income from agriculture than from herding, cattle are nevertheless the measure of wealth, success, and power. The majority of Africans are not herders. In some African cultures cattle are an important form of wealth, as among the Tiv of central Nigeria, but not so important as they are in the herding cultures of east Africa. This section is an account of major features which are common to a number of tribal groups and does not attempt to touch on specific variations (such, for instance, as the fact that bridewealth among the Nuer conveys rights of paternity but is not considered recompense for the wife herself). I use the "anthropological" present tense throughout although some of the statements are not now so true of some of the peoples of the area as they would have been some years ago. The importance of cattle today is, however, well attested by recent reports of anthropologists.[7]

In many cattle cultures the women "marry out" of their lineage, going to reside with the husband's lineage. A major element in the negotiation of a marriage between the lineages (the man and the women may have something to do with the choice, but it is also an arrangement between kin groups) is the

---

[7]A.Hingston Quiggin, *Survey of Primitive Money*, p. 26.

negotiation of the bridewealth to be handed over by the groom's lineage to the bride's lineage either before the marriage, at the time it takes place, or over a period of time thereafter. The negotiations are carried on "in principle" in terms of cattle but involve other items that can be substituted for cows, bulls, and oxen. In east Africa one finds goats and iron hoes "substituted" for a number of the cattle. Among some, the marriage-with-its-bridewealth is regarded as a completed transaction. Among others, the ideal is a two-way movement of women between the lineages and the cattle are thought of as "earnest money" guaranteeing the union until such time as a woman be sent by the groom's lineage to the bride's lineage.

The payment of cattle by the groom's kin group to the bride's kinsmen has been said to pay for the loss of the women's services to her kin. Certainly they lose her labor services, but when one spells out the consequences of the payment, both the necessary and the conditional consequences, a lot more is paid for—and a lot less, since the marriage agreement is revocable. First, the payment of bridewealth makes the offspring of the marriage a member of the husband's kin group—it "legitimizes" patrilineal descent and provides the husband's lineage with future generations of men. Second, because the bride's kin group must return the cattle if the marriage is dissolved, it often acts as a positive incentive to the bride's kin group to persuade the woman to stay with her husband. Third, it is a symbolic, ceremonial, public, honor-involved reinforcement of the affinal (in-law) bond created by the marriage; and in social systems organized primarily by kinship relations, this means it also reinforces the political alliance formed by the marriage. *What* has been bought is not a woman, as one could buy a "wench" in the United States before the Civil War, but an ongoing place for a kinship group in ongoing social relations: female labor, yes, but also sons (future herdsmen and warriors), allies, daughters (future alliances). *Who* has made the payment is the groom's kinsmen, *not* the groom as an individual (who does not "own" the cattle used in payment). The payment is made *when* the groom's kin and the bride's kin want a marriage alliance with all it entails. *How* is the payment made? Through preliminary contacts, then open negotiation of the amount of the bridewealth; in the form of cattle but also with the possibility of substituting goats or iron hoes for some cattle; and with varying systems of spacing the delivery of the bridewealth over time (hence with possible later arguments about whether the specific beasts are in fact of the quality agreed upon).

When there is a killing (both of the kind we would call murder and the kind we would call accidental homicide), lineages will negotiate a payment by the killer's kinsmen to the victim's kinsmen to recompense the latter and to avert the otherwise certain bloodfeud vengeance upon someone of the killer's lineage. *What* is paid for? Peace with honor. *Who* pays? The kin. *When*? After a killing. *How*? By transferring cattle or other stuff (goats, iron, cowrie shells). Can an individual pay in advance for the privilege of killing someone he does not like, as an American firm can buy a ton of wheat for future delivery? Certainly not—no more than I can pay a fine in advance and then freely and dangerously race my car down city streets.

Similar to bloodwealth payments are payments of cattle (and their substitutes) by an offender's kinsmen when there has been a breach of rules. Adultery can lead to such compensatory fines, as can other insults, or bodily injury or threats thereof.

Cattle may be exchanged to establish an alliance or friendship; and a friendship may be used to ask for a cow or ox of a particular sort needed in a ceremony immediately, with the promise of returning a cow (often a heifer) at a later date.

Similar to such exchanges, but sometimes with a clear implication of superiority and inferiority, important and powerful men will grant less powerful men the possession and care of some cattle—"lend" them. The recipient has the use of the cattle while in his possession: the milk; among those who bleed cattle, the blood for food; the dung; sometimes a share in the growth in the size of the herd. What is bought? Care of the herd; a reduction in the possibility that a local epidemic will kill all a man's cattle, or that they will all be stolen; disguise of the total number a man owns; the loyalty of the recipient; support in warfare; the prestige of having followers. The payment, however, is not one which ends an obligation but one which creates obligations, and it is eventually reversed when the "lender" calls in his cattle, or when his heirs call them in after the "lender's" death. In the past, among some of those east African peoples who had quasi-state systems, such lending of cattle was used in a manner much like the granting of manorial lands in medieval Europe. The political system could be described as "cattle feudalism."

To make payments such as these one must be a leader of a lineage, a chief, an important man. Such a man, acting for his group, could "buy a future for his lineage," security of person and property for his lineage, political power and prestige. He could not, however, use the cattle to buy land, which was not owned in our sense, nor for sale. The recipient of the payment could not freely use the cattle for his own purposes. The bride's lineage had to maintain the herd in case return of the bridewealth was required; the grantee of the care of cattle had to keep the cattle until the grantor asked for them back. In fact, if one of the animals paid died prematurely, the payer would have to replace it, as he might if a heifer turned out to be sterile. As a money, cattle were hedged about by limitations: on the status of the payer and payee, on the circumstances in which payment could be made, on the uses to which the cattle taken in payment might be put.

The use of cattle in these three ways does open the possibility of quantitative comparisons. Two bridewealth payments can be compared; a bridewealth payment can be compared numerically with a bloodwealth payment; and any number of either or both can be compared with the wealth (the size of a herd) of a lineage or a chief. Each is "valued" in cattle and so "cattle" are a standard of value—a *numéraire* for comparing similar but different events (marriages) or for comparing unlike events and traits (marriages and killings and prestige). But the ability to relate values—my killings were bigger than your marriages—did not mean the cattle were a medium of exchange such that I could sell sisters and daughters in order to acquire cattle with which to pay for my gloriously sadistic rampages.

## Monies: Can Use vs. Must Use

It is notable that the peoples discussed in this chapter could use their monies in a variety of ways, and had to use their monies when marrying, but that only among the Kapauku is it reported that they had to use their monies to survive. Pospisil says that families without enough land, and without the shell money to buy or rent land, went without food. Since men could be apprenticed to others and be fed and supported in the marriage game by their patrons, it is not entirely clear from the account whether a family had to have money or whether some families chose to do without rather than attach themselves to a leader (or whether the leaders would have naught to do with these families for other reasons). But in the other cases people did not *have to have* money. The necessities for survival, even the material requisites of the average standard of life for the group, were to be had without money. Money would buy food, but relatives or patron superiors would feed one. Money would buy help in farming, but relatives or age-mates would do the work. One could labor, hunt, herd, or fish for food; chop and plait for housing; stitch or weave for clothing. Money was a necessity if one wanted to enjoy the thrills of power, of being admired, of being feared, and at least once in a lifetime if one wanted to have a wife to brew or weed or feed the pigs; but it was not a necessity in order to eat, sleep, dress, and dance as others.

## Cowries, Beads, and Coins

In time and space the most common stuffs of which money has been made have been shells, beads, and metals. Of all shells, the one with the most widespread distribution, from the Pacific Islands through China, India, Anglo-Saxon graves, and Africa to the western hemisphere has been the cowrie. "The original occupant of this solid, shiny, slightly symmetrical shell with its narrow ventral opening was a gasteropod mollusc living in shallow water and preferring the water to be warm, hence its distribution in the Indian and Pacific oceans."[8] The *Cypraea moneta* is a bit over an inch long, the *Cypraea annulus* a bit less than an inch long. Both are the shape of a

---

[8]For this and the previous paragraph see Quiggin, pp. 25-44. For an analysis of the roles of cowries, see Polanyi, *Dahomey and the Slave Trade*, Chapter 10 (extremely difficult) and Chapter 11; these are reprinted in George Dalton, editor, *Primitive, Archaic, and Modern Economies: Essays of Karl Polanyi*, pp. 261-305.

somewhat elongated or pinched egg, and the shape with its opening is sufficiently reminiscent of the primary female organ to warrant viewing it as a fertility charm. With the back of the shell pierced the vent permits stringing the cowries. Unstrung they are easily countable, the best cowrie counters of west Africa being able to count piles of over 100,000. As a money they have one other very definite advantage: they are unmistakable and uncounterfeitable.

There were and are beads, beads, beads. There are "aggry" beads of unknown origin found in the earth in Africa. There are trade beads of modern industrial manufacture. Beads, like the cowrie, are used in trade, used as money, and often given the benefit of belief that they have some magical powers as well as innate beauty. And like the cowrie, their use is worldwide.

Then there have been and are coins. Lumps of silver stamped with a device have been found in Mesopotamian sites dating from 2,000 years B.C. The first clearly authenticated coins stamped by public authority are those of the Greek kingdom of Lydia in northern Asia Minor, in the seventh century B.C. These were made of electrum (an alloy of gold and silver occurring naturally in the streams of Lydia). Since then there have been a great variety of coins: of gold, of silver, of brass, of copper, and very often of alloys of silver and copper. Coins have been minted by kings and emperors, by towns and by privileged nobles granted the right to mint, and by others who assumed or usurped the right to mint.

Unlike cowries and beads—a cowrie is a cowrie and a bead is a bead— coins in use have merged with the metal of which they are made. Silver measured by weight was used in the eastern Mediteranean world before it was stamped "as a coin," and coins were long weighed and assayed in order to evaluate them at their silver or gold content rather than at the value stamped on their face. When central banks of countries pay each other in gold today they do so in gold bars, not in coins. Public authorities have stamped coins to guarantee their weight and fineness (purity of the metal), and public authorities have used the stamp to pass off coins of precious metal adulterated with base metals or slightly underweight. Some coinage has been "full-bodied": that is, of metallic value equal to its face value. Some coinage has purported to be "full-bodied" but has been beneath standard in weight and fineness. Other coinage, like all coinage today, has been "token" coinage, that is, a convenience which is not supposed to be of much metallic value.

The presence of coins or cowries or beads tells us little about the organization of an economy or about the role of money in the economy. Certainly it does tell us that there were payments made in coin or cowrie or bead, but it does not tell us who used the money for what; whether the money was essential to livelihood in that society; whether much or little work got done or whether many or few goods were acquired in exchange for the precious metals, cowries, or beads. Were they the "money of kings" or the "money of everyman"? Sometimes they were the money of the great; sometimes the money of the masses; sometimes essential, sometimes not.

# V

## MONEY IN THE MIDDLE AGES AND THE MERCANTILIST PERIOD

### Medieval Manors

From the seventh to the fifteenth centuries the unit of political, social, and economic organization in which most Europeans lived was the manor, going under various names according to locality, history, and language. From the Islamic conquest of the eastern and southern Mediterannean in the eighth century until the eleventh and twelfth centuries there were few towns and these were small. There was little commerce until the tenth and eleventh centuries; piracy restricted trade to the south and east, Vikings of un-Christian bent terrorized and pillaged to the north and east. Without a strong successor to the centralized administration of imperial Rome there was neither maintenance of roads nor protection from brigands (the more success-ful of whom became nobles without acquiring a sense later called noblesse oblige), and there were few coins.

Most people were attached to a manor. Probably no more than a tenth of the population lived in towns, even during the heyday of the towns in the thirteenth to fifteenth centuries. Venice with 100,000 people was huge; Ghent with 50,000 was very large. Commonly towns had 5,000 to 10,000 people; and towns were mostly situated along the great north-south trade routes.

The manor was an area—ranging from less than a square mile to a few square miles—assigned to a noble by his overlord for the noble's support in war and administration. Over the centuries lands were given to the church in order to support good works, to glorify God, and to prove the piety of the donor. There were many great estates comprising a number of manors, often scattered, but the world within which most people lived was a manor, belonging either to a lord or to the church. On it lived the servile families who tilled the arable land, grazed the livestock, and engaged in rudimentary handicraft production—the people we call serfs. In characterizing the medieval manor one must do all sorts of injustice to variations. Some people associated with a manor were freemen. The degrees and kinds of servility, the dates at which earlier freedoms were lost and later freedoms gained—all these varied. The manorial system of Franco-German ninth-century Europe did not spread to Scandinavia, and manorial serfdom came late to Russia, only in the sixteenth and seventeenth centuries. The great, middling, and petty nobles of France and Germany had rights, and especially effective powers, against their kings and Holy Roman Emperors that English nobles never enjoyed *vis-à-vis* an English king after 1066. Early pioneering agricultural colonists in the Low Countries (now Belgium and the Netherlands) were free in a way in which the humbler classes of France and Spain were not until the eighteenth and nineteenth centuries.

Serfs were born to their status and could not leave the land. They devoted part of their effort to tilling strips of land in a grain-grain-fallow or grain-fallow rotation; part to tilling the domainal land of the lord; part to caring for pigs, sheep, cattle, and chickens; and part to weaving, milling, and cottage building. The domainal land, whose produce was reserved for the lord, was tilled as one of the obligations the unfree serf owed the lord. Such items as eggs, meat, firewood, linsey-woolsey cloth, and butter were supplied to the lord as his dues. The lord or his bailiff in turn administered justice, according to the "custom of the manor" and his own powers and proclivities, and supported men-at-arms who together with the lord protected the servile population from marauding brigands and avaricious neighboring lords. The manor was a largely self-sufficient unit. Salt had to be brought in from outside, as did iron products. Luxuries for the lord, and the better sorts of weapons, were also brought from outside, along with spices and some wines. But most calories eaten, most proteins and fats eaten, most cloth worn, most rushes strewn on the floor, most trenchers for holding food, most wood and mud and brick for building (lovely stone castles were few)—most of the material wherewithals of life were produced and consumed on the manor. The distribution of the products of the manor depended neither on sale nor on barter. The lord, his bailiff, and his other retainers got their wherewithals in kind, delivered by the serfs from the product of the domainal lands or from the dues of the serfs (tribute might be the best general word for these "donations") and the serfs got their specialized services from the miller or blacksmith and donated to their support, typically a share of the milled wheat going to the miller and another to the lord. Small local markets existed, but these were not essential for everyday support for serf or lord. They provided a social occasion, an opportunity to sell some petty extra or to buy one.

There were rules—the "custom of the manor"—that governed who did what, who got what: a status of some sort for those who abided by the rules and a chop of some sort for those who did not. The small silver coin of the time, the penny or denarius, was one 1/240th of a pound of silver—except that it was much more often than not more copper than silver. Coins were always welcomed and could always be used; but they were few and seldom if ever needed. Access to land, and the getting of food, clothing, shelter, beer, wives, husbands, salvation, protection, and justice depended upon the status of the person and the common understanding of how the local customs of the manor applied to each person.

In this "system of householding in kind," money in the abstract had a role. When dues were expressed in money they were often paid in grain or work or eggs. Rights over land owned by the free were sold and bought, but there was not much land owned by freemen. Land held by grant from the lord's overlord, whether by hereditary right or not, could not be transferred without the overlord's permission, and most transfers were by inheritance or were gifts to the church. When there was a need to compensate someone with a right to inherit in some circumstances or a right to some of the product of the land, the obligation to pay was often expressed in money terms—pounds, shillings, groats, dinars—but payment was made with a horse or a saddle or some furs.

Livelihood for those on the manor did not depend on the sale of produce. When a sale of some produce not needed for the sustenance of a peasant's family or the maintenance of a lord and his entourage could be made, serf or lord was happy to get money. But until the tenth and eleventh centuries there were no markets large enough to make production for sale a possible way to earn a living. As towns grew they provided markets for the products of the countryside, but only of the countryside near the towns. Only when crops failed and famine threatened, usually a result of the ravages of war, was it worthwhile to move foodstuffs long distances.

## Medieval Towns

The town economies were different. They were centers of commercial trade and steadily growing manufactures. Incomes in towns were received in money from the sale of goods transported and sold in long-distance trade or manufactured and sold, and from wages. The everyday goods of life, food and clothing, the services of masons and carpenters—nearly all the necessities as well as the luxuries of life—were bought. Within the towns and their surrounding areas, the petty coinage of the town was used for daily trans-actions.

The towns were the centers and way-stations of long-distance trade. The continental cities bordering on the North Sea and the Hanseatic cities of northern Germany traded to the Baltic for furs, for grain, and for iron, and to

England for wool. The cities of northern Italy traded to the east for spices, semitropical foods, silk, and cottons. There was a flow from east and south Asia through the Islamic countries to the Levant shores of the Mediteranean, and thence to the towns of northern Italy. Over the Alps or up the Rhone and down the Rhine, the trade finally reached Flanders and the north. The products of the north, especially woolens in increasing quantities, flowed in the reverse direction. This was a trade in luxury or semiluxury goods: things of high value relative to weight. (Common folk did not wear woolens, let alone silks, but linsey-woolsey, a roughly spun and woven mixture of linen and wool. As late as the early eighteenth century cotton was a luxury item, servant girls being warned against the offensiveness of their daring to wear cotton stockings.) It was a trade for the benefit of the wealthier nobles, the prelates of the church, and the merchant traders themselves. The manufactures of the towns were also luxury goods. Most of Europe was rural and feudal, and towns an exception.

## Medieval Monies

Three sorts of monetary systems may be distinguished in the medieval world. First there was the local currency, largely a token currency in fact if not in name. Constantly adulterated and depreciating, these token currencies were used for wages and for daily purchases in the town markets. Of little value as metal, local currencies tended to stay within a small area.

The second sort of money was also a currency, for interregional and intercity trade, and might be called an international currency. Before the conquests of Islam the gold *solidus* of Constantinople was *the* coin. After the Islamic conquests gold virtually disappeared from medieval Europe; silver became the stuff of coinage. But for a long period there was not much in the way of an interregional, intercity money. Charlemagne's currency of a pound, divided into 20 sous or shillings or into 240 denarii or pence, was a hypothetical pound, and the shillings were hypothetical too. The only actual coins were the penny and the half penny. It was a coinage for petty trade, for the almost self-sufficient manorial life. With the revival of commerce in the tenth century there came the development of a variety of heavier coins: Arab gold dinars, Persian silver dirhems, and then in the thirteenth century the famous coinages of the Italian cities: the florin of Florence, the ducat of Venice. The gold weight of these coins was about four times the weight of gold which a United States dollar would have purchased in the 1950's. Obviously, they were the coins of aristocrats, merchants, and long-distance trade. Earlier in the thirteenth century came a silver coin for commerce: the Venetian groat which was the model for the French gros (or *sou*; German *groschen*) and the English sterling (shilling) coinage. These were the coins whose weight and fineness were maintained for long periods and were preferred by payees.

The third system has been called "imaginary money,"[1] "ghost money,"[2] and "money of account." In a physical sense it did not exist; in a commercial sense it was a major money. There were the full-bodied coins of international commerce and there were the coins made of silver alloyed with copper and of pure copper used for petty local trade and wages. The relationships between the values of gold and silver changed, it is true, but at nothing like the frequency and rate at which the exchange rate between the petty coinage and the grand coinage could change. In consequence one of two things happened in commercial accounts. Either (1) accounts were kept in physically real local pennies and imaginary or ghost shillings and pounds or (2) accounts were kept in physically real florins and in ghost shillings and pence.

In the first case ultimate payments of larger sums would be made in actual coins (groats, florins, ducats) at current rates of exchange with the hypothetical pound, the rate deriving from the actual, debased penny. In the second case ultimate payments of small sums would be made in actual pennies, the rate depending upon the relationship between the hypothetical penny of the real florin and the real debased penny. In origin the ghost pound descended from the hypothetical pound of Charlemagne, while the ghost shillings and pence of the real florin descended from periods at which the relationship between the petty and the grand coinage had been stable. In Milan, for instance, in the last half of the fourteenth century, a florin exchanged for 384 pennies. This florin and the pennies were material. Between the two denominations were 32 imaginary shillings of 12 material pence ($32 \times 12 = 384$); 20 of these imaginary shillings constituted an imaginary pound, equal also to 240 of the material pence. When at the beginning of the fifteenth century the price of the florin in Milan began its rise to 768 actual pennies in 1445, the florin of 384 pennies became a ghost, but a real ghost. It was, like a ghost, immaterial; but like a proper ghost, everyone believed in it and used it in accounts. Conversely, when at the end of the thirteenth century a period of a stable rate between actual florins and actual pennies ended, the Florentines kept the florin physical and continued to use ghost shillings and pence, 29 ghost shillings or 348 pennies to a florin. (Medieval Europe was not unique in having imaginary monies. In nineteenth-century Canada, for example, where the fur trade had long been carried on in kind, the unit of the "skin" was used in accounting and statement of debts. The "skin" referred to no particular kind of pelt but was equated with fifty

[1]Luigi Einaudi, "The Theory of Imaginary Money from Charlemagne to the French Revolution," in Frederic C. Lane and Jelle C. Riemersma, editors, *Enterprise and Secular Change*, pp. 229-261.

[2]Carlo M. Cipolla, *Money, Prices, and Civilization in the Mediterranean World, Fifth to Seventeenth Century*, pp. 38-51.

cents, and the values of various kinds of actual pelts were expressed in multiples and fractions of the imaginary skin.)

The situation required money-changers. We today require money-changing from dollars to pounds to francs to marks, and banks engaged in international finance do it for us. But the medieval merchant or financier did not use one money here (florins) and another money there (ducats) but used several monies every place he dealt: gold coins, silver coins, petty coinage. And the gold and silver coins were not simple, whole multiples of each other. If the florin and ducat and groat had a fine career of constant weight and fineness, there were many less stable-valued coins minted by sovereigns or private people to whom the right of minting had been granted. These others often debased the coinage by adding alloys, and there was constant clipping —paring slight amounts of metal off the edges of the coins. (Milling coins to raise and corrugate their edges to prevent clipping dates only from the seventeenth century.)

Standards of deferred payments were not necessarily the media of exchange, and many could not be because they were ghosts. Means of payment were often monies, but a mixture of monies which bore varying relationships to each other. Gold and silver were stores of value, but not so much because they were money as because they were treasured. Imaginary monies also served as stores of value for creditors, in the accounts owed to them.

## Debt and Credit Instruments

A common form of payment among medieval merchants was the bill of exchange. This was a promise to pay a sum in a particular money at a particular place—generally not the place where the bill was written—at a specified future date. The bill had several advantages for those in commerce. First, it reduced the need to transport valuable coins, a costly business both because transport was expensive and because of the ever present danger of brigandage. Second, it was a means of extending credit—lending and borrowing—between the time at which an obligation arose and a more convenient time for payment. Third, it provided ways around prohibitions upon the charging of interest. At the fairs of Champagne (twelfth into fourteenth century, on the north-south trade route) the Church's prohibition of usury (charging any interest at all, in those times) was suspended, and maximum rates of interest set. But in other dealings the differences between the monies, and the question of the proper exchange rates among them, would, could, and did "hide" an element of usury.

The medieval bill of exchange had much in common with modern bills in form, but lacked negotiability.* A bill promising payment at a future time

---

*See the discussion of negotiable instruments in Chapter VI.

could be collected only under the law of agency by any person other than the original creditor—that is, only by an agent acting for the benefit of the creditor. Furthermore, the principals (Original Creditor and Original Debtor) or their agents had to be present. This requirement made it extremely difficult to sell the bill to third parties, although efforts to get around the law, such as by giving power of attorney for one transaction only, were made. The result was that a creditor could not sell an IOU (bill) to a third party who could sell it to a fourth party. This in turn meant that the IOU of Debtor could not be pledged as security by Creditor with a third party because that third party could not collect on the IOU, except most cumbersomely as agent-attorney for Creditor. The third party could not sell the IOU to a fourth party to recoup his loss if Original Creditor failed to repay his borrowings from Third Party. Two essential elements of modern money and banking were therefore lacking from medieval practice: checks, and lending on discount or against trade bills. Practices, and the legal rules that followed the development of new practices, slowly changed, but it was not until the beginning of the eighteenth century that the modern law of negotiability emerged firmly and clearly.

## Bullion, Money, and Mercantilism

In rough coincidence—at least in the century or so centering around the year 1500—three major and interacting changes took place in European society. There were (1) the discoveries of the New World and the sea routes to south, southeast, and east Asia, with the associated shift of the centers of commerce from Italy and decline of the European north-south route with the rise of the Atlantic routes; (2) the emergence of the nation-state; and (3) the Protestant Reformation.*

The conquest of Central and South America brought huge quantities of silver to Europe (the great raids of Francis Drake and Henry Morgan were for silver, not gold; the mines of Latin America were mostly silver mines). This silver not only eased a European "money problem," which had been an increasing shortage of precious metals for coinage, but it also led to a long period of price inflation as the influx of silver exceeded the expansion of the need for silver in commerce. However, the development of the nation-state and of the trade with Asia created two new monetary problems, which were in turn compounded by the absence of a simple means of multilaterally offsetting debts among the merchants and the emerging nations of western Europe. The problems were: (1) the need of a nation-state for money to pay a professional army and bureaucracy; and (2) the need of merchants for silver to pay for imports from Asia.

---

*There is a literature arguing for and against the thesis that Protestantism was an important element in furthering the rise of capitalism. With that issue we need not deal here. The effect of the Reformation upon the building of nation states was, if nothing else, to make the struggles between them terribly cruel and bloody until the end of the Thirty Years' War in 1648.

## Money for Domestic Needs

Ever since Adam Smith criticized the mercantilists—the merchants and statesmen of the sixteenth through eighteenth centuries—it has been common to say that they naively confused precious metals with the wealth of a nation, which truly lay and lies in the productivity of a nation's resources and population. To confuse the amount of silver in England with the standard of living of the average Englishman was foolish, as Adam Smith saw—just as it would be foolish to confuse the amount of gold in Fort Knox with the standard of living of the typical American in the 1970's. But the mercantilists were not that dumb, no dumber than the modern financier who worries about the loss of United States gold reserves. The modern financier does not think that gold within the boundaries of the United States makes General Motors and TVA productive. He worries about the breakdown of a system of payments between countries which allows the United States to import goods and raw materials with ease, regularity, and security. Similarly, the mercantilists were worried about the breakdown of their systems of government and trade.*

The medieval system of government had been one which delegated much —in some places almost all—of the administration of justice and maintenance of order to the nobility, who derived their material means from the manors allotted to them. These nobles, the baronial and knightly vassals of king, duke, and count, provided the armies of medieval Europe. As part of the oath of fealty to his lord the vassal promised to supply himself and a number of fighting men, typically for forty days a year, to his lord for the conduct of his lord's wars. In effect, the "pay of the army" was the granting of manors to vassals.

The emerging national governments—identified with king-and-crown in Spain and France, identified with crown-and-parliament in England and the Netherlands—wanted civil servants and armed services which depended directly and entirely upon the central government. Only then could the feudal nobles be disciplined by the nation-state. It was the lands and the powers granted to the nobles in the feudal system which allowed them to defy the king.

The new solution was to pay the judges and civil servants and soldiers and sailors of the new nations in money. There were, however, no national monetary systems such as we have today: payees did not want verbal or paper promises from kings or parliaments; trusting neither kings nor parliaments,

---

*In defense of Adam Smith it should be said that he was arguing against corruption and incompetence in the civil services of the late eighteenth century, against a background in which international monetary affairs ran more smoothly than earlier; and, most importantly, he was arguing for a new and better way to run the world. Therefore, one can admire Smith for his aims and foresight, while recognizing that his and subsequent treatments of the mercantilists were poor history.

payees wanted coins, and they did not mean copper coins. Whatever the productivity of Newcastle mines or Yorkshire sheep or the merchants of Hull and London, what the government of England needed in order to rule was silver. Hence one reason for the emphasis on silver.

The government could lay hands on silver irregularly by sending a Francis Drake off to rob the papist dogs of Spain, but a more assured supply would be forthcoming from taxes paid at ports of import; and if there were not much silver within the kingdom it would not be possible to collect other taxes in silver. Therefore the governments supported the idea that the balance of trade should be "favorable"—that more silver should flow in than out. Adam Smith argued that the purchasing power of a single coin when there was a small supply of coinage would be proportionally high and hence wages could be lower in silver by weight. But that argument would not in fact have satisfied rebellious Scottish highlanders, Dutch allies, or German mercenaries. Similar thoughts in similar circumstances occurred to kings of France.

## Money for World Trade

The eastern trade around the Cape of Good Hope and via the Baltic through Russia to China required silver. The peoples of the east were not much interested in buying European goods, either British woolens or Dutch salt fish. What they wanted was silver, for treasure hoards and for jewelry. There was thus an inevitable net drain of silver from Europe to the orient. This meant that a nation and its merchants must have a net inflow of silver from other trade, or else be unable to buy in the oriental trade. The mercantilists were not wrong when they thought that one man's gain was another man's loss: if the Amsterdam merchants had the silver and the London merchants did not, then the Amsterdam merchants got the eastern goods and the London merchants did not.[3] Two centuries from now, when solar energy is harnessed directly, some critical clown will come along and say that people in the late twentieth century confused petroleum with transportation. Obviously, we do not. But equally obviously, our system of transportation comes to a standstill when we lack oil and gasoline. So too, many kinds of trade in the mercantilist period came to a halt when buyers lacked silver.

The problem was compounded by the absence of a system of multilateral international clearings through which net credits in one intra-European or North or South American or African trade could be set off against net debts in another trade. Had the nations and merchants of the time been able to set off the surplus in one trade against the deficit in another by bookkeeping transfers, as we do today, then much less silver would have been needed to make

---

[3]This problem and the difficulties of offsetting credits and debts, discussed in the next paragraph, are covered in Charles Wilson, "Treasure and Trade Balances: The Mercantilist Problem," reprinted in Lane and Riemersma, *Enterprise and Secular Change*, pp. 337-349.

up the final balance than was needed when each trade had to be financed separately.* The restrictions on the negotiability of debts (IOUs) made private offsetting of surpluses and deficits difficult to impossible.

Many modern attitudes toward money stem from this mercantilist period, reenforced by experiences of intervening years. More than in medieval Europe—where ghost monies of account were common and payments were made in pepper, cloth, oxen, horses, furs, and vases and any other things acceptable to the payee—silver (or gold) was needed in mercantilist Europe of the sixteenth through eighteenth centuries. One cannot have a pig feast with goat meat, and Charles II and Louis XIV could not conduct a war with copper coins and paper bills.

---

*Under the nineteenth-century gold standard, enormously increasing volumes of trade were financed not by paying in gold but by dealing in credit in the London money market. Since World War II the amount of gold has not increased much, but international trade has. New York and London, and more recently European centers of finance, aided by the International Monetary Fund, have financed the growth of trade with little movement of gold. We now seem to be in process of developing a system of payments in which international promises made through the IMF—known as special drawing rights, familiarly called SDRs or "paper gold"—will allow settlement of international debts without any movement of any money stuff.

# VI

## PROMISES, PROMISES, NOTHING BUT PROMISES

The origins of modern money—money as we know it and use it today in the industrialized societies of the world—can certainly be traced back to the coinage of the ancient world and to the forms of commercial debt and early banks of deposit of the medieval world. Our continued use today of "deposit" stems from the first bankers who received and kept in strong boxes the monies of depositors. But the monies we use today began to take on their present forms in the eighteenth and nineteenth centuries, and these are largely the product of the development of commercial banking.

### Negotiable Instruments

Commercial banking required the development of negotiable instruments. A negotiable instrument is a piece of paper which has three characteristics: (1) it is evidence of a right, or of a claim against others; (2) it can be transferred by the owner to a third party without the consent of the organization or person against whom the owner has a claim; and (3) it endows the third party with all the rights and powers with which it endowed the preceding owner.

The most common example today of a negotiable instrument is the check. A check is an order by the customer-depositor to his bank to pay—to himself, to someone else, or as the someone else directs ("to the order of"). Legally a check is a shorthand form of a letter which might read "Dear Bank, on this 10th day of May, 1979, I order you to pay Joe Zilch, or to whomsoever he orders you to pay it, the sum of fifty dollars. I guarantee to Joe Zilch, and to whomsoever else may come into possession of this order by endorsement, that Bank will make the payment, and if Bank fails in this duty, then I shall make the payment. Sincerely, Walter C. Neale."

56

Another negotiable instrument is the "bill." A manufacturer (or whole-saler) ships goods to the purchaser, and along with the goods goes a "bill." The purchaser writes "accepted" on it, signs it, and returns it to his supplier. The "bill" when sent to the purchaser was a "You Owe Me"; once signed by the buyer it becomes an IOU. The supplier can take this "bill"—now variously called an "acceptance" (because "accepted"), a "trade bill" (be-cause "guaranteed" by the existence of the goods shipped in "trade"), a "commercial bill" (for the obvious reason), or "two-name paper" (because signed, and therefore guaranteed, by both the seller and the buyer)—to his banker and "discount" it. The supplier of the goods takes the accepted bill to his banker, who extends credit—gives money to the supplier—against the supplier's IOU with the bill as security. The transaction is called "discount-ing" because the amount of money provided by the banker is the face amount of the supplier's IOU less a charge that is in effect the interest. Thus on a bill for $1,000 payable at the end of 90 days the banker will advance to the supplier (the banker's customer-borrower), say, $980. This deduction (dis-count) of $20 is the equivalent at an annual rate of $80, and is expressed as a discount at a rate of 8 percent per year. When the bill becomes payable, the purchaser of the goods pays the supplier and the supplier pays his bank $1,000. Bills are discounted as a rule for 60 or 90 days, but upon occasion, as with bills arising from the shipment of agricultural produce, for as long as a year.

Such bills were the foundation of commercial banking. Commercial banks, of which there were not many before the nineteenth century, were established to finance "commerce"—that is, the shipping and selling of goods. When a manufacturer or plantation owner shipped goods, the buying merchant or processor often lacked the ready cash or other means to pay for the goods on receipt and wanted credit until he had received money from the sale or further processing and sale of the goods. The shipper (a manufacturer, other merchant, plantation owner) needed to pay his ongoing costs of opera-tion and he likewise often lacked the ready cash or other means of payment. The commercial bank lent money to the shipper so that the shipper could extend credit to the buyer until such time as the buyer had realized money from his subsequent sales and could pay the shipper (who could then repay the banker). It was felt that the existence of the goods "guaranteed" or "sup-ported" the repayment of the loan. The goods would be sold (or the possessor of the goods could be forced to sell the goods), so that getting the money to repay the loans of bank to shipper and of shipper to buyer would be almost automatic.

Of course, if the market value of the goods fell during the period of shipment and while being held for sale, then the receipts would not cover the outstanding debt; but this was a recognized risk of commerce, and good judgment and profits on other loans and on other transactions of the borrowers were supposed to make up for the risk. Moreover, both the borrower and his debtor were responsible for paying the bank. In the financial panics of the nineteenth century (and to a lesser degree of the twentieth century) many borrowers and bankers could not make up for their errors of judgment and went bankrupt—but fortunately for the development of modern money and finance, hope sprang eternal.

The monthly charges consumers get from department stores, telephone companies, and public utilities are called "bills" because they have the same root meaning. However, they differ from commercial bills in that they are bills for goods which will not be resold and therefore banks would not discount them if one were to write "accepted" on them and mail them back to the store.

The development of the law of negotiable instruments was crucial to the development of modern money and banking on two sides. First, banks became willing to lend against the security of a negotiable instrument because a bank could collect the debt evidenced by the negotiable instrument if the debtor failed to pay. Furthermore, a bank could itself sell the negotiable instrument to a fourth party if the bank decided it wanted another kind of asset. Second, negotiability made it possible for nonbankers as well as bankers—for every person or organization with an account at a bank—to pay by writing checks against bank accounts, a process possible only when each successive possessor-by-endorsement could collect the debt evidenced by the check.

Originally, banks provided credit for the conduct of commerce; in these beginnings, discounted trade bills were the major money-earning assets of banks. As land became more freely saleable, with the disappearance of feudal restraints on the transfer of land, banks lent on mortgage. Nineteenth-century mortgages were, however, for only a few years. Then, over the years, with growth of large-scale corporate industry, with the development of other kinds of IOUs (especially corporate bonds), and with the enormous growth of government demand for loans, banks have undertaken to offer many other kinds of finance and today the commercial bill against goods in transit is a small portion of total banking business.

The borrowers, who are debtors to the banks, are one kind of bank customer. Creditors, whom we call "depositors," are the other kind of bank customer. A depositor owns a promise by his bank to pay him. These deposit-promises come in two forms: "demand deposits," which we also call "checking accounts"; and "time deposits," which we also call "savings accounts" (and of which there are numerous classes). Demand deposits are promises by a bank to pay whomever, however, and whenever ordered by the depositor. Time or savings deposits are also promises by a bank to pay the depositor, but with restrictions on the timing and method of paying. Deposits are overwhelmingly the major liabilities of banks.

What a bank promises to pay is "so many dollars" or other appropriate national monetary units. How the bank fulfills its promise is up to the payee, whether the payee be the depositor or the person or organization to whom the depositor has ordered that the payment be made. A payee may insist on being paid in legal tender—that is, in coins or in paper money, the offer of which has been declared by the national government sufficient to fulfill an obligation to pay money owed ("all debts public and private," as it says on United States paper money). But usually the dollars are considered paid when an entry is made in the books of the payee's bank crediting the payee (the recipient of a check) with that amount of dollars; thus a new promise to pay the payee has been substituted for the old promise to pay the check writer. The system of payment of money in a modern economy will be explained below in the sections on Clearings and Creating Money; for the moment, it may be mentioned that payment in currency is a very small proportion of all payments made in a modern, industrialized economy. The common mode of payment is by transferring title to deposits from payer to payee, and this is accomplished by the negotiable instrument called a "check."

What "backs" these deposit-promises-to-pay? In one sense the promises to pay are backed by the assets of the bank, which assets are largely in the form of promises by borrowers to pay the bank. Only a very small percentage of the assets—equal to only a very small percentage (only 2 to 4 percent) of the deposit-promises—are in the form of currency (coins and engraved paper money). In this sense promises by businesses, governments, and mortgagors are what back the promises of the bank to pay. In another sense the law of contract backs the promises to pay. If the bank cannot fulfill its promises to pay it can be forced to go out of business. A court-appointed "receiver" will then sell the bank assets, or sell the bank-with-its-assets as a going concern, and will pay the depositors as much of what is owed them as can be realized from the sales. (In the United States today most bank deposits are insured by the Federal Deposit Insurance Corporation, so that for deposits up to $40,000 Americans do not need to worry.)

It is often said that the banking system works because only a few people want to withdraw their money at any one time. Although the statement is true, if "money" means "currency," it misconceives the processes involved in banking. A banking system works because mostly people do not want to "withdraw money"—meaning currency—but want to order their bankers to make payments which can be made (and payees prefer them to be made) by reducing the deposit of the payer at his bank and increasing the deposit of the payee at his bank. People, businesses, and governments do not withdraw currency in significant quantity but instead transfer among themselves the debts of banks—the demand deposits banks have promised to pay. In so far as currency is withdrawn from banks it is as rapidly redeposited in banks by the recipients of payments-in-currency. But if one asks the question "What would happen if all depositors ask for currency at the same time?'' the answer is simply: ''Our banking system would collapse.''

The assets of a commercial bank are of three sorts: (1) physical equipment; (2) earning financial assets; and (3) nonearning financial assets. The latter two are the interesting ones; the physical assets are a ''mere necessity''—a place to conduct business, with walls and vaults and pens and tellers' cages.

Earning assets have been described. Nonearning financial assets have taken a number of forms over the course of banking history. These are the assets which usually fulfill the bank's promises ''to pay on demand to the order of.'' One group consists of what we would all recognize as money: gold coins, silver coins, copper coins, nickel and other base-metal coins, and the ''folding stuff'' (engraved with pictures, numbers, and words we seldom read). Another group consists of non-interest-bearing claims against other banking institutions, the demand deposits of one bank at other banks.

The commercial bank is in business for profit and its profits come from interest on the loans it makes and the bonds it has bought. These earning assets are of several sorts, although all have in common the essential characteristic that they are IOUs of some borrower. Any bank would rather own such an IOU which pays it interest than own a nonearning asset, hence will hold only as much of its total assets in nonearning forms as it feels it must to fulfill its promises—except in those cases where it cannot find a suitable credit-worthy borrower or acquire suitable income-earning assets. (An actual bank statement of assets and liabilities is reproduced in the Appendix at the end of this chapter, with explanatory notes on the meaning of the terms used.)

## Banks, Money, and Means of Payment

Although the conscious intent of the banker is to earn interest on loans, a commercial bank in our modern monetary system has two further major and more important functions. One is to clear (that is, to offset) counterbalancing debts; the other is to ''create'' (and to destroy) money by lending (and by being repaid). It is the clearing function which permits banks to create money, and it is the danger of being unable to satisfy creditors in the process of clearing which restrains banks from ''creating'' an unlimited supply of money. The world of commercial banks (and of modern money) is a world of clerical operations, faith, judgment, and (largely) fulfilled expectations. How does this world work?

First one should ask, ''What induces a bank to make promises to pay on demand and to accept such impolitely worded orders as one finds printed on a check?'' Either one of two reasons. First, the bank—call it Bank A—has earlier received a ''deposit'' from the customer-depositor, most likely in the form of a check which was an order by a third party to Bank A or to another bank to pay to the customer-depositor. Thereupon: (1) If the check were an order to Bank A, Bank A fulfilled its old promise by making a new promise to the customer-depositor. (2) If the check were an order to another bank—the expression is "drawn on" another bank—then Bank A would take the check in exchange for its own promise to pay its customer-depositor on demand because it can use the check to clear against (offset) checks drawn against itself and deposited at other banks. (There are, of course, some further inducements to the bank: it is going to collect service charges against small customer-depositors in the United States; it is lending for interest to many of its larger customer-depositors; and when minimum balances are kept to avoid service charges the bank has been able to use that amount of deposited checks in clearings without having had to clear checks against the unused minimum balance.)

The second reason why a bank makes a promise to pay is that the bank receives, in exchange for its own promise to pay any time (a loan) a promise to pay the sum plus interest at a future date from the customer-borrower. This customer is both a debtor-as-borrower from the bank until the loan plus interest is repaid and a creditor-as-depositor of the bank as the recipient of the loan. The loan by the bank takes the form of a credit entry added to the demand deposit of the borrower (which is "creating money," as will be explained below).

What a bank has promised to do for its customer-depositors is to pay as they order. What does "pay" mean in this context? It means, as it has meant elsewhere and at other times, to turn over "something" which the payee is willing to accept in payment. It may (but these payments involve petty amounts in terms of the total payments made) pay out currency from the teller's cage. It may (but again the amount as a proportion of total payments made is small) pay by deducting the ordered amount from the account of one customer-depositor and adding it to the account of another customer-depositor. But mostly banks pay each other: Bank A pays Bank B when Bank B has come into possession by deposit of a check drawn against Bank A. If Bank B were willing to accept 100 dozen eggs in payment there is no legal objection to its doing so; but banks-as-payees are not satisfied with eggs and want something else—a "money" that they can use in fulfilling their own promises to pay. What are acceptable (satisfying) forms of payment? (1) Currency, but currency is bulky to transport (compared to a single piece of paper), and expensive to transport because armored cars and guards must be paid for to protect the bundle. (2) Deposits at another bank. These are the preferred means of net payment. Such deposits may be at the creditor bank; at a clearing house (see below); or at a third bank (which is what United States Federal Reserve Banks are). (3) Deposits at the debtor bank itself, which it would otherwise have to pay in forms (1) or (2). Insofar as this third method can be used no further crediting/debiting or moving or coins and paper money is needed. However, other banks are unlikely for long to accept a bank's promise to pay in payment for that same bank's promise to pay.

## Clearings

A clearing house (a joint organization of a number of banks in an area) provides the facilities for setting off against each other the checks drawn on one bank and deposited in other banks and the checks drawn on other banks and deposited in the one bank. Each bank, at the end of its banking day, brings to the clearing house all the checks it has received in deposit which have been drawn on the other banks. For each bank the total of these checks is what the other banks will owe it—the credit side of its balance with the clearing house. Then all the checks brought in are sorted into groups according to the bank against which the checks were drawn and the total in each group is the amount which each bank owes the clearing house. The difference between a bank's claims against other banks and all other banks' claims against itself is the net amount of payment which must be made, either by the bank to the clearing house (called an "adverse clearing") or by the clearing house to the bank (called a "favorable clearing"). The net debts may be carried over from day to day at the cost to the debtor bank of interest charges; they may be paid by a check drawn on a third bank. So long as the volumes of checks "payable to" and "payable by" each bank equal each other over a period of several days the promise of one bank to pay is fulfilled by setting off that promise against the promises of other banks to pay. No "somethings" other than the cleared checks change hands.

In a clearing operation there are actually *two* monies—closely related monies, it is true, but nevertheless two monies. One is the money expressed on the cleared checks: the common, everyday money which people and businesses use to pay each other. The other is the bankers' money: the credit balance at the clearing house which the banks are willing to accept in payment. A dollar (a pound, a franc) of "everyday" money exchanges at 1:1 (equality) with a bankers' dollar, but families and businesses never see, never use the bankers' clearing house money (not any more; but before World War I, for instance, New York City Clearing House bills circulated as money when the "everyday" stuff was in short supply). For many purposes a distinction between a dollar of "everyday" money and a dollar of bankers' money, which exchange for each other at 1:1, is pointless. But when "everyday" money is in short supply bankers can create their own interbank clearing-house money by allowing each other to carry forward larger day-to-day debts. Conversely, the clearing house, if it has authority to act independently of the member banks (as, for instance, the United States Federal Reserve Banks have), can reduce or limit the amount, uses, or costs to the banks of banker's money.

## Creating Money

So long as a bank can make all the payments it has promised to make it is fulfilling its obligations and can continue to stay in business lending at interest. The danger to a bank is that it will suffer a run of adverse clearings and that the other banks and/or the clearing house will refuse to accept its promises to the clearing house, or that the clearing house (including central banks) will cease to extend credit to cover the adverse clearings. Then, in the absence of a supply of coin and engraved paper money and in the face of refusals to accept eggs in payment, the bank must close its doors. But this will only happen if the volume of clearings against a bank is rising faster than the volume of clearings against other banks. If the volume of clearings against each bank is rising at the same rate, the total clearings will continue to offset each other and no bank will need to close its doors.

What will make the volume of clearings against a bank rise? For one thing, a larger volume of business involves the depositing at other banks of more checks drawn by the bank's customer-depositors. But in such a case other checks deposited by its customer-depositors will often offset the larger volume of checks which are drawn against the bank. Clearings against the bank will also rise if the bank lends more money, a process which consists of a bank taking an IOU from a customer-borrower, adding the IOU to its assets (under the classification "loans"), and crediting the customer-borrower in his other role of customer-depositor with a larger demand deposit. The borrower (unless he is a nut who is willing to pay interest to see large numbers on his bank statement) is going to spend this loan—pay it out to other people and businesses who will in turn deposit his checks at their own banks. The checks will clear against the lending bank and the lending bank will find itself suffering a series of adverse clearings—*unless* other banks are simultaneously making more loans, in which case the total volume of checks cleared against them will also rise and the net adverse and favorable clearings will still fluctuate around zero, each bank "paying as promised" by clearing against others. As the volume of loans increases, so step by step does the volume of demand deposits.

Economists call this process "money creation." Why?

Because banks create money freely at will on their own? No. Banks create demand deposits (that is, they promise to pay customers on customer's demand) and we the public—individuals, businesses, government agencies—accept these promises of banks in payment of obligations. When the payee's bank accepts the payer's check in a clearing, the payee is satisfied that he has been paid. The payee accepts the demand deposit as money, and therefore it is money—it is an acceptable means of payment. Neither the banks nor the government forces us to accept payment in demand deposits, and each of us does have the right to insist on payment in legal tender (engraved paper money in most of the world today); but we usually accept demand deposits in payment. So in a very important way it is not "at the will" of the banks that demand-deposit money is created but "at the acceptance by many payees." And banks cannot create money "freely" because they must be able to honor their promises. In our money and banking system this means with coins and engraved paper, with acceptable checks on other banks, or with acceptable credit at the clearing house. Therefore a bank will not lend more and more ("Whoopee, the sky's the limit!") unless it is assured that it will have the means of honoring its promises. It will be so assured when more deposits are made with it—when its clearings are running favorably and it is running up favorable balances at the clearing house (or, much less importantly, amassing currency in its vaults). Even if a bank has only a very little means of payment acceptable to other banks and not immediately needed to meet adverse clearings (that is, if it has only slightly favorable clearings over a few days), it can increase its loans slightly and still cover any resulting small adverse clearings. These adverse clearings will be favorable clearings for other banks which can increase their loans (and thereby demand deposits). Each bank will receive "more money" from other banks at the same time as it is paying out "more money" to other banks; thus the clearings for each bank will continue to average out to zero over several days. And in this sense banks lend only money which they have received in deposit; the "gimmick" is that the "money" received by each bank is the "promise to pay" of another bank, and so long as the promises offset each other there is no "day of reckoning."

What then stops banks from increasing loans and demand deposits to infinity? Aside from the fact that the banks want to be repaid by borrowers and there is not an infinite supply of good-credit-risk borrowers who will repay, two things have historically stopped banks from lending. (1) In the first half to three-quarters of the nineteenth century (and until later in the United States) banks would call upon each other for payment in gold (or silver) and people and businesses would withdraw and use more gold and silver money as incomes and prices rose, leaving banks without or with smaller amounts of acceptable means of payment. This was called "the cash drain." (2) The monetary authorities (usually the central bank in each country) can sell assets it holds (usually bonds issued by the government) so that all other banks suffer adverse clearings and only the central bank enjoys a favorable clearing. In these circumstances the central bank can insist that the other banks lend less and reduce the volume of demand deposits—and central banks do so in order to limit the amount of money available as means of payment.

## A Consequence of Bank Money

A major consequence of the development of commercial banking and demand deposits is that money-made-of-a-money-stuff has become much less important than it has been at other times and places. Most modern money does not "exist" in the sense that a physical item—a rock, a coin, a child, a cow—exists. It does exist in a sense perhaps somewhat analogous to the sense in which a marriage exists. Both, at least, are promises: money the promise of a bank to pay on demand; marriage the promises of husband and wife to love

and support each other. There are records of both: of money in the banks'
ledgers and in your and my files of bankbooks, canceled checks, and bank
statements; of marriage in the license office, perhaps in the church records,
and sometimes in the family Bible. Both involve public authority: the promises of the bank can be enforced in the courts, and the bank forced out of
business if it does not fulfill its promises; the obligations of a marriage can be
enforced in the courts (child support) and the spouse can be forced out of a
marriage (divorced) if he or she does not love and behave properly.

## Modern Money Is Different

Two characteristics of modern economies create a role and a power for
money which is lacking in societies with other, more limited-purpose monies.
One characteristic is the wide variety of things and services which can be
bought with money and the purchase of which requires only the consent of a
single seller (as opposed to situations in which several independent parties
must agree, as is the case with the purchase of much of the land in medieval
Europe, or with the payment of bloodwealth where that occurs). The other
characteristic is that our money can be and is created whenever a bank agrees
to exchange its promise to pay (which demand deposit is money) for the
promise of a borrower to pay in the future. Together the two characteristics
allow a business organization to get control of an enormous quantity of
productive resources. The resources are for sale by their owners: land and the
minerals and fuels in the land; labor and skills embodied in people; buildings,
machines, and all sorts of other products. To buy these resources one does not
need first to save or to gather together existing money items in order to use
them for payment. In Kapaukuland one needs shells to buy pigs, but in the
United States one needs only to persuade a banker to create the money to buy
land or machines or to hire labor. Availability of the needed inputs for
purchase plus money creation allows participants in a monetized economy to
rearrange the uses we make of man and nature and to change the distribution
of wealth and income within society. The railway network built in the
nineteenth century was not paid for with money put aside by savers to buy
land and rails and engines but instead with money created by the banking
system and spent to buy land and labor and iron and coal away from other
uses. IBM did not grow because Mr. Watson and people who bought IBM
stock paid for a concern the present size of IBM, but because IBM used bank
money to buy inputs in much larger quantities than the original stockholders
and subsequent profits could have financed. Had modern corporations waited
upon savings in coin or silver certificates by others willing to buy their stocks
and bonds or upon piling up coins and silver certificates out of profits, they
would never have attained to their present size, and it is doubtful—although it
cannot be proved either way—that the industrialized countries of the world
would have amassed anything like their present productive capacity.

This situation contrasts with the situations one finds in many other systems with money. Where payments are made in cows or cowries, pigs or silver coins, then the capacity to pay, to fulfill obligations, to purchase inputs (if they are in fact available for purchase) requires that first one get one's hands upon the actual, existing cows or coins. One can, of course, borrow the cows or coins, but to borrow twenty cows or ten thousand cowries one must first find a person or persons with twenty cows or ten thousand cowries and then deliver the cows or cowries to the creditor or seller. One can promise to deliver the cows in the future, and such promises do allow people in money systems tightly tied to physical money items to make payments in excess of the actual physical items available, but the accounts we have of special-purpose monies seem to portray systems in which the actual items rather than the promises to pay them make up the substance of the monetary system. Whereas the accounts do imply, at least, that the total number of "pigs" owned in Oceania at any time exceeded the number of actual pigs, the pig debts—the promises to pay—did not themselves circulate as negotiable instruments equivalent to money. One cannot, in Oceania or East Africa, borrow promises to deliver money items and then use these promises to buy power and prestige; but what a modern corporation does when it goes to banks to borrow money to build factories is precisely to borrow promises which will give it control over great quantities of productive inputs.

In pre-industrial societies the range of things which could be purchased has been limited—in part because some useful things were simply not for sale and in part because the technology of the societies could not produce a large variety of goods. The range has also been limited because the geographical areas involved tended to be small. In contrast, modern industrial societies produce thousands upon thousands of different things. Most of them are for sale; and the variety is much increased by the fact that things can be bought in all regions of the world. The consequence is that money can be and is used in the creation of new industries, in the transformation of populations from farmers into industrial laborers, in the development of massive corporate empires. People and organizations with access to bank credit—those to whom banks are willing to lend—can amass means of production which make their owners very rich and which can change the centers of economic and political power within and between countries.

**APPENDIX: A Bank's Balance Sheet, with Explanatory Notes***

THE PARK NATIONAL BANK, KNOXVILLE, TENNESSEE
Statement of Condition—June 30, 1974

*Note*

| | | |
|---|---|---|
| (1) | **RESOURCES** | |
| (2) | Cash on Hand, in Federal Reserve Banks and Due from Banks .................................. | $ 43,696,914.45 |
| (3) | Federal Funds Sold ................................ | 45,000,000.00 |
| (4) | U.S. Government Obligations ........................ | 34,331,088.52 |
| (4) | Bonds of Government Agencies ..................... | 7,502,373.47 |
| (4) | State, County and Municipal Bonds (fully guaranteed by U.S. Government) .............. | 18,159,438.10 |
| (4) | State, County and Municipal Bonds .................. | 16,433,773.38 |
| | (TOTAL OF ABOVE)............................. | $165,123,587.92 |
| (4) | Loans and Discounts (Includes Mortgage Notes—Farmers Home Administration) .............. | 112,858,265.46 |
| (5) | Stock in Federal Reserve Bank ..................... | 330,000.00 |
| | Banking Houses, Furniture and Fixtures (9 Offices) ...................................... | 7,569,729.19 |
| | Interest Earned—Not Collected ...................... | 1,790,308.67 |
| (6) | Customers' Liability on Letters of Credit .............. | 568,479.95 |
| | Other Assets (Prepaid Insurance, Expenses, etc.) ................................ | 103,580.03 |
| | **TOTAL RESOURCES** ........................... | $288,343,951.22 |
| | **LIABILITIES** | |
| | Capital Stock ..................................... | $ 3,000,000.00 |
| | Surplus .......................................... | 8,000,000.00 |
| | Undivided Profits ................................. | 5,675,857.32 |
| (7) | (TOTAL OF ABOVE) ........................... | $ 16,675,857.32 |
| (8) | Reserves ......................................... | 1,789,648.79 |
| | Allocated Reserves (for Taxes Interest, etc.) ................................... | 2,929,279.76 |
| | Interest Collected—Not Earned ...................... | 5,984,441.99 |
| (6) | Letters of Credit Outstanding ...................... | 568,479.95 |
| (3) | Federal Funds Purchased (Handled as Agent for Correspondent Banks and included in Federal Funds Sold) ........... | 32,800,000.00 |
| (9) | **DEPOSITS** ...................................... | 227,596,243.41 |
| | **TOTAL LIABILITIES** ........................... | $288,343,951.22 |

*Reproduced by courtesy of the Park National Bank of Knoxville, Tennessee. The Notes are not part of Park National Bank's statement of condition.—WCN

*Explanatory Notes*

(1) "Resources" is another name for "Assets."

(2) About one-third of this sum is the bank's reserve deposit at the Federal Reserve Bank. Most of the rest consists of deposits at correspondent banks in New York, Chicago, and a few other cities.

(3) Balances with Federal Reserve Banks not needed for clearing on June 30/July 1 and lent for one day to banks in need of reserves for anticipated adverse clearings. Other banks, with immediate need for more liquidity, would show a lower figure for "Federal Funds Sold" (asset) than for "Federal Funds Purchased" (liability).

(4) Earning assets of the bank: debts of governments and government agencies and of private individuals and companies to the bank, on which the debtors pay interest. Note that over 81 percent of total assets consists of earning financial assets, and that about 15 percent of total assets consists of currency and of deposits with other banks.

(5) The banks which are members of the Federal Reserve System "own" the Federal Reserve Bank of their district—"own" in quotation marks because the important decisions of the Federal Reserve System are made by the Board of Governors of the System, appointed by the President of the United States. The member banks do receive dividends of 6 percent on their stockholdings in the Federal Reserve Bank.

(6) Letters of credit: guaranteeing letters issued by the bank to those of its customers who wish to get credit where they are not known. As an asset the letter of credit is debt of the customer to the bank as soon as the customer presents the letter elsewhere. As a liability, it is Park National Bank's debt to the distant bank which extends credit to Park's customer.

(7) The sum of these three items plus Reserves (see Note #8) is the "net worth" of the bank: the amount by which its assets (what is owned by or owed to the bank) exceeds its liabilities to others. The division into four classifications is a consequence of laws governing incorporation, banking regulations, and accounting procedures and does not affect the value of the bank to its owners.

(8) The United States Internal Revenue Service allows banks to deduct from taxable profits small amounts to allow for bad debts and other unforeseen contingencies. The amount shown is the sum of all such allowances made in the past, adjusted for actual bad debts never recovered. It appears separately from the other three classifications of net worth as a result of United States tax laws. These reserves have nothing to do with the bank's reserve deposit at the Federal Reserve Bank (see Note #2).

(9) This total is made up of about $69 million of demand deposits owed to individuals and businesses; about $104 million of savings deposits owed to individuals and businesses; about $21 million of demand deposits owed to other banks; about $32 million of demand and savings deposits owed to state

and local governments and public agencies; and $1 million owed to the United States government. Very roughly, about half of the deposits are demand deposits. Note that 78 percent of the sum of net worth and liabilities to others consists of deposits. Note also that the means of payment immediately available at the opening of business on July 1—the sum of "Cash on Hand" plus "Federal Funds Sold" minus "Federal Funds Purchased," or $55.9 million—amounted to less than 25 percent of deposits, and under half of demand deposits. It is the earning assets, the wisdom of bankers, and the law of contract which underlie our system of money and banking.

This statement of assets and liabilities shows that Park National Bank is managed conservatively. Loans and discounts are the assets which are difficult to sell to third parties, so a low "loans to deposits" ratio means high liquidity, or ability to get generally acceptable means of payment quickly. The bank's ratio of 44 percent was unusually low for a United States bank in 1974. The same conservatism is evidenced by the fact that easily marketable bonds of governments and their agencies constitute 40 percent of the bank's earning assets (other than Federal Funds).

# VII

## THE EMERGENCE OF MODERN MONIES

### Bank Monies

Modern banks did not arise quickly upon the development of the law of negotiability. What negotiability of promises did was open a number of possibilities to people and to governments, whereafter people and governments tried out the possibilities, some with more and some with less success.

The stimuli to invention of money devices and money processes were twofold. On the one hand there was the steady expansion of the volume of commerce, requiring increasing amounts of means of payment; on the other hand there were the needs of governments, particularly pressing in times of war and political crisis.

There has never been enough money, in the sense that there have always been people and organizations who could see very good uses for more money if they could lay hands on it. Since money came into general use, this has always been true of princes and governments (and accounts for the earlier debasement of metallic currencies). During the eighteenth century the lack of money to pay became increasingly felt by those engaged in commerce, and during the eighteenth and nineteenth centuries by those engaged in manufacturing.

Discounting of bills of trade increased the means of payment available to the commercial community so long as people were willing to hold bills rather than ask for the silver or gold coinage which everyone thought of as "really money." And because discounting provided an interest income for those who held bills rather than coin, there were people willing to hold bills. A Virginia plantation owner could discount his bill for shipping his tobacco to England, use the credit entry with his English banker to buy crinolines and silver snuff boxes, and repay his banker (cover the discounted bill) with the draft (an early form of check) he received when the tobacco was sold. The plantation owner never needed to see coin in these transactions. The seamen who worked the ship and the weavers who made the crinoline wanted coins—real money—to pay the grog shop and the grocer, but the need for coin as a proportion of the total finance was reduced.

Even so, the need for a circulating medium of exchange increased. If promises on paper signed by shipper and consignee could circulate among the members of the business and financial communities, why not circulate "one-name" paper signed by a reputable person among these communities and the whole population? The bearer (he who had in his hand the "one-name" paper) became, as a result of negotiability, the creditor of the issuer of the paper. No one had to accept such a piece of paper, but if people would accept it, why not issue it? Such issuing would further reduce the need for coins of precious metal. And even though many people were not enthusiastic about taking paper instead of coin, paper was better than nothing to use in payment. Issued in volume by bankers, one-name promises to pay were printed and became known as "banknotes"—notes of debts payable on demand by the issuing banker.

Typically a banknote read that the directors of the bank promised to pay the bearer on demand a named number of pounds in gold coins (Britain) or a named number of dollars or francs in gold or silver coins (United States and France). In the early nineteenth century, any bank could issue its own "banknotes," although with some restrictions (for instance, the Bank of England had a monopoly on the issue of banknotes within 65 miles of London). Banknotes are similar to demand deposits in that they were a promise to pay by a bank, and differed in that the bearer (whoever was in the possession of the banknote) can demand payment from the issuing bank, whereas only the owner of a demand deposit or the persons (or organizations) specifically entered on the face of his check or endorsed on its back can make this demand. Banknotes were *not* usually legal tender (although some were—Bank of England notes after 1833). They did, however, circulate widely, constituting a sizable portion of the currency supply. Demand deposits were not used nearly as much in the first half as they were in the second half of the nineteenth century (by businesses and relatively rich people; it is only in the twentieth century that they have become a common means of payment for many people). Instead of paying by check it was common in the first half of the nineteenth century to draw banknotes from one's bank and make payments with these banknotes. If the recipient of a banknote (the payee in a transaction) so wished, he could go to the bank that issued the note and demand coins of precious metal (although, where a paper money had been given the status of legal tender by the state, the issuing bank could pay in such legal tender—Bank of England notes, United States "greenbacks").

Banknotes differ from coins and from the monies printed by governments and given legal-tender status in that while they are an asset of any other bank coming into possession of them, they are a liability of the issuing bank. In this respect they are equivalent to the demand deposits of one bank at another bank.

Banknotes gave rise to problems. Within a smallish area around the issuing bank, where the credibility of that bank's promises was common, the banknote was accepted at face value. When the banks were big and widely known (the Bank of England, or the first or second Banks of the United States, for instance) their banknotes would be accepted nationwide. However, a banknote issued by a small bank in Lancashire would not be immediately recognizable as "good" in London. The doubts in Philadelphia, New York, and Boston about notes issued in Knoxville, Tennessee, and Peoria, Illinois, would be greater.

What happened when a bank in Peoria failed to honor its banknotes, when it went bankrupt and could not pay 100 cents on the dollar to its creditors? Or, more commonly, when it "overissued" its banknotes and could not fulfill its promise to pay in silver and gold coin when asked to pay? Answer: the holders of the banknotes lost some to all of the face value of the banknotes. The consequence was that banknotes often circulated "at a discount," meaning that they were accepted in payment at less than face value; or alternatively, one had to pay a higher price, if paying with these notes, than one did if paying with silver or gold coins or with banknotes which were known to be good.

Obviously this was a fine system for those who borrowed from banks and spent the banknotes to bid for the resources they wanted, or to repay debts they had incurred to others. Equally obviously, those who found themselves holding discounted notes, and notes which were increasingly discounted, felt that they had been "ripped off."

Banknotes were not the only private obligations that were accepted as money in payment. As the need for a circulating medium of exchange grew with the expansion of industry, while the supply of small coins for daily use did not increase so rapidly, manufacturers produced token coinages with which to pay their employees. These circulated, for instance, in the early nineteenth century in the newly industrializing area of Lancashire. When the Prussian government was successful in controlling the extension of credit and thereby in limiting the new bank money, bankers in neighboring German states issued fictitious bills which circulated as a medium of exchange and means of payment in Prussia.

## Government Monies

Governments have had an advantage over private organizations in creating more means of payment. In the middle ages, princes could make a limited supply of silver stretch farther by adding copper to the mix. Later governments could issue "fiat money" (that is, pieces of paper declared "legal tender," sometimes for making payments to the government and sometimes for paying "all debts, public and private"). The phrase "legal tender" means that the courts of the nation will rule that a debt is paid if the debtor turns over, or presents to turn over even if refused, the sum due in "legal tender." The "greenback"—properly known as the "United States note"—is an example.

The real horror stories about bad money come from earlier periods, from the 1923 hyperinflation in Germany, and from the hyperinflations in China and Hungary after World War II. In the eighteenth-century cases, there was usually an effort to link the fiat money to some asset or expected revenue which would bring in the "real money" to redeem the fiat government notes. John Law's scheme in the 1730's (to issue a paper currency backed by the expected profits of France's Mississippi possessions) anticipated the economic development of the region by almost a century, too long to ask note users to keep their faith. The French revolutionary governments after 1789 issued "assignats," fiat money to be redeemed from the proceeds of sales of land confiscated from the nobility. The revolutionary government's need for means of payment outran the amount of such land and even the area of France, had it all been for sale, and the assignats depreciated to a few percent of face value.

Britain's North American colonies, like all governments of the mercantilist and immediately postmercantilist period, were hard pressed for means of payment. British credit was fine for plantation owners and exporters of salt fish; it did not provide Pennsylvania and Rhode Island governments with coins to pay the militia. The colonial governments therefore issued "bills of credit"—fiat money "backed" by anticipated tax revenues or by anticipated receipts from repayment of loans made to farmers against mortgages on their lands. Where the issues were limited, as in Pennsylvania, their purchasing power was maintained and they served well as means of payment. Where, as in Massachusetts, need or desire for means of payment overbore restraint, the bills of credit depreciated. The problem was not that the Mississippi valley did not produce profits or that the Commonwealth of Massachusetts was delinquent in levying and collecting taxes. The problem was that governments issued means of payment faster than the demand of the commercial, industrial, farming, and financial sectors of the economy for those means of payment rose. In contrast, the United States government issued "unbacked" greenbacks for decades without their losing purchasing power. "Unbacked" legal-tender Bank of England notes circulated with increasing purchasing power as British governments followed generally deflationary policies after World War I.

It is sometimes said that the governments did not learn the proper lesson: that any means of payment will work if limited in amount and no means of payment will work if issued too freely. Actually, the lesson was learned by governments: ask any smoker if he knows that cigarettes are dangerous to his health. Certainly the lesson was learned by others. The gold standard and bimetallism were the ways to prevent governments from overissuing paper money; the paper money was to be always and *immediately* redeemable in gold, or in gold or silver. The gold or bimetallic standards also disciplined bankers, who under them were required to pay in gold, or in gold or silver, on demand.

Hence the two reasons given to justify the gold standard: (1) to save us from the avarice of governments; and (2) to save us from the idiocy of bankers. So closely similar were the problems of fiat money and of banknotes that avarice and idiocy can be substituted each for the other in either of the two suggested reasons.

## Limiting the Private Power to Promise

The history of money in the nineteenth century was in large part the story of the attempts by public authorities to control private organizations' use of the power to create means of payment. Another large part of the story was the efforts by private organizations and public-spirited citizens to limit governments' abilities to use the power to mint or print legal tender.

Government policies to restrain the private economy's creation of means of payment were first directed toward making all banknotes easily redeemable at par in precious metals. In addition, in order to protect the "little man" where banknote issues were not well controlled, banknotes were limited to large denominations so that only those "who should know better" would be stuck with them. Later the power to issue banknotes was limited or abolished: in England by giving the monopoly of the note issue to the Bank of England; in the United States by allowing only federally chartered ("national") banks to issue Treasury-printed "national banknotes" and these only up to 90 percent of the face value of United States government bonds which the banks had to deposit as security with the Treasury.

Finally, partly in response to financial crises (to "do something" quickly) and partly by conscious legislation, "central banks" appeared in all countries. In Britain the Bank of England was originally chartered in 1694 in a deal whereby the merchants of London made a loan to William of Orange to finance his war with France in return for a monopoly of joint-stock (corporate, limited-liability) banking in England. During the Napoleonic Wars it became the main source of the paper money in those years, and during the 1850's and 1860's evolved techniques for helping to tide solvent but illiquid*

---

*A firm is solvent if its assets exceed its liabilities. A firm is nevertheless illiquid if its demand debts demanded exceed its immediately available acceptable means of payment.

financial institutions over financial crises by providing them with Bank of England credit (that is, with a bankers' or money-market money) while simultaneously restraining the total supply of means of payment.

Other European countries established central banks in the latter part of the nineteenth century; in some cases the large bank which had been the government's bank took on the duties of a central bank. In 1913 the United States Congress established the Federal Reserve System as a decentralized central bank, but by 1934 the importance of New York as *the* center of finance and the New Deal reforms of that year gave the United States a proper central bank.

### What Is a Central Bank?

A central bank is now often defined as the monetary authority responsible for regulating the supply of money in order to help to maintain a condition of full employment without inflation. In the nineteenth century it was defined as a "lender of last resort"—the monetary authority responsible for providing enough "bankers' money" to prevent widespread failure of financial institutions and the collapse of the money-and-banking system while simultaneously limiting the total amount of money so that the nation's currency would not lose purchasing power in international trade and finance.

More generally, a central bank might be defined as a bank so large, with so many financial assets to sell, and with so much capacity to create acceptable means of payment, that by itself it can force almost all other banks into adverse clearings with itself, or by itself assure almost all other banks of favorable clearings. In the former case, it makes other banks reduce the amount of credit (that is, the amount of money) they provide, which means the central bank can limit the means of payment. In the latter case, it allows the banks to lend more, thereby increasing the available means of payment.

How it uses this power has varied over the past century and a half. One thing has always been true: that with the power inherent in its size, a central bank has always had to be responsive to the values and aims of the nation. What the public purposes have been has changed. For two decades the Bank of England helped finance Britain's wars with revolutionary and Napoleonic France. In the 1850's and 1860's it emerged as the recognized central bank of Britain by protecting London's financial institutions in times of domestic and international financial panic. In the 1920's the mission of each central bank was to maintain the purchasing power of its nation's currency in terms of other nations' currencies—an aim which was then perceived as identical with the preservation of the gold standard. After the experience of the depression of the 1930's, the public purpose of central banks was to restrict or enlarge the availability of means of payment in order to restrain or encourage spending in order to maintain full employment without inflation. Modern central banks can do much to help achieve the Utopia of a job for everyone while maintaining yesterdays' prices at the grocery, but they cannot do it alone since they must fit themselves to other public purposes as well. The governors of the Bank of England, the Federal Reserve Bank of the United States, and the Reserve Bank of India are like elders in an African cattle culture. Elders can affect bloodwealth and bridewealth, but they cannot survive as elders if they disgrace clans' dignity or brides' families, nor can they prevent the promise of nine goats from substituting for two cows. Governors can limit the means of payment, but not if doing so offends workers in Detroit or closes banks in Boston. Governors and elders differ in that the money the governors affect affects the livelihood of us all, whereas the elders affect the dignities of some far more than they affect the availability of goods to all.

# VIII

## THE IMPACT OF MULTIPURPOSE MONEY
## ON TRIBAL SOCIETIES

There have been many societies in which the money has had a limited role. Modern multipurpose money, however, is a powerful social device. It can play an important part in creative activities and it can expand the effective freedom of individuals. It can also be destructive of social relationships, helping to introduce changes faster than members of a society can adapt their ideas and social processes to the changes. Two cases—one involving European rule and settlement, the other European rule only—illustrate the potential power of multipurpose money. Some similar cases also exhibit these disintegrating effects.

### The Case of British Central Africa

The idea of money and dependence upon a monetized system to organize the production and distribution of goods had a major role in the economic and social history of British Central Africa—what is now Rhodesia, Zambia, and Malawi.[1] The Pioneers, as the conquering settlers from South Africa and Britain were called, had a mental picture of an economy and social system in which people produced goods for sale for money; in which the organizers of production hired labor for wage payments in money; in which everyone bought what they needed to survive, or to enjoy, with the money they

---

[1] An exciting account of the period 1890-1920 is Philip Mason, *The Birth of a Dilemma*. For the interwar period see Godfrey Wilson and Monica Wilson, *An Essay on the Economics of Detribalization in Northern Rhodesia*, and Margaret Read, "Migrant Labour in Africa and Its Effects on Tribal Life." For the period of colonial rule after 1945 see William J. Barber, *The Economy of British Central Africa*.

received from sales of produce or from wages earned working for others; and in which the costs of government were paid for with money that had been collected as taxes. In this view of how the world worked it was almost—not quite, but almost—inconceivable that anyone would not work for money or would not sell what he produced for money. In the Pioneers' view an offer of a money wage would "naturally" call forth a supply of willing workers, eager for the money which they could use to buy daily necessities and the other goods that make life more pleasant. Coming as they did from a society that had been thoroughly commercialized for generations, one in which a working class had to have wage employment and since the early nineteenth century had been demanding it, the Pioneers were taking a view of the way the world worked that was quite consistent with all they had experienced. It was also, in their view, the way in which all economies ought to work. Thus the Pioneers' view of the economy was not much different from that held today by most Americans and Europeans; it differed only in their growing conviction of their own racial, cultural, and religious superiority.

The Bantu peoples whom the Pioneers conquered and among whom they settled had different views—not just different views about what ought to be, but about what in fact was. With debt in the sense of obligation the Bantu were familiar. They were of course familiar with the use of cattle or of iron in making payments to establish marital ties and to settle disputes. But coined and paper monies were something new.

Money as the Pioneers conceived it was part of a larger system of economy and society, and this system too was foreign to the Bantu. Land, for instance, was not a saleable property belonging to this or that individual Bantu or his immediate family; rather, it was the surface of the earth over which people moved, settling here or there for a while, cultivating the land until its productivity declined, and moving on. The tribal area did belong to the tribe in the sense that it was not for the use of people from other tribes, insofar as the tribe was strong enough to hold it against others who came to seize them and their cattle and foodstocks. But within the tribe land was assigned to lineages, to kraal groups, and within the kraals (the separate settlements) to heads of families who assigned areas to wives to cultivate. One did not buy land; one was granted or allowed or told (the choice of verb is irrelevant here) to cultivate an area of land. When one left one did not sell the land. There were no buyers; the land was becoming exhausted anyway—that is why the group was moving on. Food was grown to eat, grain to brew into beer to drink. Livestock was bred and herded for its milk, hides, and meat, and sometimes its blood. Among some tribes the cattle were the source and sign of prestige and power. But no one sold land, nor did people or kin groups or tribes sell cattle. Cattle were bred to get more cattle, not to sell. A person would work for or with another because she was a wife, because she was a co-wife of the other, because he was related to another, because he or she lived in the same kraal with another, because he was a member of the same "age set" as another, because he acquired prestige and protection in return for herding another's cattle, or perhaps because he feared the other. Men—"by their very nature," a Bantu might have said—herded, fought, and cut and burned brush on new land. Women planted, hoed, and reaped.

Quite aside from the issue of who was to rule Central Africa and get the larger share of what Central Africa produced, the situation of two cultures living in the same area with two different views of how things were done must inevitably have created conflict, disruption, and change in both societies.

The immediate needs of the Pioneers were for land and the labor to make that land productive. Conquest provided the Pioneers with the land, although even the taking of the land was not, in the Pioneers' view, a case of armed robbery. Rather, the Pioneers saw land which was not being used, land which in European terminology would have been called unoccupied waste—the sort of forest and swamp land into which their ancestors had moved and had reclaimed; or they saw land used by nobody and belonging to nobody, certainly nobody in particular. Labor was another matter. Slavery, seizing local people and forcing them to work on the land, had become reprehensible in European eyes, and if the Pioneers themselves were not so particular about the lines between wage labor, forced labor, and slavery, the people of Britain and the Colonial Office clearly disapproved of all slavery. In any case, in the beginning the Pioneers assumed—it seemed obvious to them—that labor would be forthcoming to work the land if wages were offered. Wages were offered, but Bantu did not come forth to work the land.

Money was, in the Pioneer view, the link between man, work, and material welfare. The links, in the Bantu view, were lineage, kraal, sex, and age group, adjusted by political power in those tribes with incipient state systems. How could a *male* be expected to cultivate? To ask such work of him was to ask for economic transvestism.

The solution imposed by the Pioneers was a requirement that a head tax be paid in money, thus requiring that Bantu work to earn the money to pay the tax. It was not a happy solution, not even from the point of view of the Pioneers. First, without a census, with the Bantu shifting about across the surface of the areas reserved for them in the division of the land after the conquest, it was impossible to levy the tax on individuals. Where there were chiefs, the administration required the chiefs to recruit the labor to earn the money to pay the head tax. Where there were no chiefs, chiefs were created. The Bantu who then came to work the land and tend the herds of the Pioneers did not work hard because they felt neither moral nor economic compunction to do so. They ran off if they dared; they left as soon as they had earned the money required to pay the tax. The Pioneers, quite rightly as they saw the world, thought the Bantu shiftless, lazy, dishonest, incompetent, and irresponsible—"childlike" in the Pioneers' phrase. The Bantu, quite rightly as they saw the world, thought the Pioneers threatening, brutal, and at least somewhat crazy.

Both cultures changed. The whites increasingly used force rather than wages to recruit labor. Legislation imposing criminal penalties reinforced wages as inducements to work. A society of Europeans which had depended on money to organize and integrate economic activity came increasingly to use force instead or in addition. A society of Europeans who had recognized class wound up creating a caste system.

The Bantu on their side found it increasingly difficult to survive in the areas assigned to them. What had been enough land at one time, when a family or clan could move to other land later, was not enough land to support tribal life over decades. And what was not enough land over decades to support shifting agriculture became much less than not enough as the Bantu population grew. Increasingly it became necessary for men to leave the reserved land to work the land of the settlers and to work in the mines of the companies in order to earn money to buy food. Migrant not settled labor became a mainstay of the Central African economy. Between the World Wars it was said of Nyasaland, now Malawi, that its "major export was men." The low wages combined with the "for men only" mining compounds in which the migrant labor lived undermined the social structure of the tribal Bantu remaining in the reserved areas. Family life was disrupted. Without enough men at time of clearing land, agricultural productivity in the reserved areas fell. Men away from their homeland for years felt put upon when they faced the demands of a multiplicity of kinsmen. Elders and leaders in the old system felt that the younger migrants lacked respect for them.

Increasingly the Bantu came to need and then to want money and the things money would buy. But at the same time they found themselves excluded from all but the lowest positions in the monetized economy. Meanwhile, what had been an effort, in line with British Colonial Office policy, to interfere as little as possible with the customs of conquered people, to reserve areas to them on which they could continue their older way of life when not engaged in the monetized economy, became a barrier to further adjustments on the part of the Bantu. Shifting cultivation and moving herds about over large areas had been a viable system of agriculture and animal husbandry when population was small relative to land area; but when population grew, the old system became an ecological disaster. Well-meant efforts by officers of the government to cull herds down to sizes the pastures would support were viewed by the Bantu as robbery. That the excess stock should be sold for slaughter was an objective of the officials, but selling livestock for strangers to kill and eat was not part of the Bantu ideas of how one did things. Nor were the material benefits which money from the sale of livestock could bring proper substitutes for the dignity which possession of large herds gave. Without tenure on particular pieces of land, without the opportunity to improve the land so that it might support continuous settled cultivation, the Bantus became less and less able to feed themselves.

To "blame it all on money" would be wrong. Ideas of property, of irrevocable contracts of sale, of the distribution of the products of the economy in accord with individual property rights and the wage bargain—all these were basic to the conflict of perceptions of what was and what ought to be, as also were ideas of race and duty and superiority and fear of the large mass of Bantu surrounding a small number of Europeans. But it is also true that money was an integral, operating part of the European system of ideas that included individual property rights and irrevocable contracts as principles and practices in economic life. And, for the Bantu, what money must buy (and then, as time passed, what money could buy) became both a necessity and a temptation in conflict with the other parts of the Bantu system of social and economic organization. While destructive of tribal life, which might be considered a "bad thing," opportunities to live a different life, to be independent were also given by the multipurpose money of the Pioneers and by the European companies' economy. Whether or not (in the eyes of European or African historians, or of that impartial Lord or Martian who will make the ultimate judgment) the necessities and the opportunities were beneficial in the long run, multipurpose money was certainly an important element in changing the lives of the descendants of both white and black in Central Africa. And it changed them in ways that differ from the ways in which, for instance, the lives of conqueror and conquered were changed in Manchu China, or in Ptolemaic Egypt after Alexander's conquest, or in Gaul and Britain after Caesar's conquest, or in Spain after the Arab conquest.

## The Case of the Tiv

The history of the impact of multipurpose money among the Tiv,[2] a tribe living in central Nigeria, differs greatly from the history of the impact of European conquest, economy, and money among the Bantu of Central Africa. Europeans never seized the land of the Tiv nor did they require labor from the Tiv. Nevertheless, a combination of British-imposed law and British-introduced multipurpose money changed Tiv social structure.

Before the 1920's the Tiv had a social system with three spheres of exchange and the Tiv of the 1950's still thought and felt in terms of those spheres. First, there was a subsistence sphere of foodstuffs, livestock other than cattle, household utensils, and the tools and raw materials with which to make them. While Tiv loved to go to market—a market was a place to meet friends and relatives, to chat, to drink, to dance—it was not necessary to go to market to eat. People produced their own subsistence, and when that was not

---

[2]See Paul and Laura Bohannan, *Tiv Economy*. For a short account, see Paul Bohannan, "The Impact of Money on an African Subsistence Economy."

enough they could ask relatives for food. When a shortage of food involved a large area, people would "send hunger" (a request for food) to relatives distantly situated.

Second, there was a prestige sphere of slaves, cattle, ritual offices, large white (*tugudu*) cloths, medicines and magic, and brass rods. In this sphere brass rods were the standard of value, the medium of exchange, and a store of value.

Finally, there was the sphere of "exchange marriage," the sphere on which most attention focused, the sphere most important to a Tiv's conception of self and society. In this sphere a man or group of men in a lineage had rights over women, rights which they exchanged in marriages for rights over other women. When the males of one group married one of their female wards to the males of another group and married one of the female wards of the other group, an "exchange marriage" had taken place and each of the two groups acquired from the other full rights in the offspring of the marriages. Marriages did not always last—women did have something to say about whether they liked their husbands, and they could elope with someone else—so that an unfulfilled debt could arise because the exchange marriage was only half completed. This debt could be paid by sending the daughter of the incomplete (called a *kem*) marriage to the other group. Meanwhile, earnest of good will and proper intent was shown by sending brass rods or cattle. In a *kem* marriage the wife was sexually and economically a member of her husband's group, but her children did not become wards of her husband's group. Each child as it was born had to be *kemmed* to affiliate it to the father's kin group. Morally, a *kem* marriage was inferior to an exchange-of-women marriage. Properly speaking, to the Tiv, the only true payment for a woman was a woman.

The Tiv ranked the spheres morally. Least worthy or interesting was the subsistence sphere; most worthy was the marriage sphere, "supreme and unique . . . for the Tiv" (p. 126 in Dalton, *Tribal and Peasant Economies*). The brass rods of the prestige or intermediate sphere were general-purpose money within that sphere, but were limited to the payment function in the other spheres. Morally "downward" in the subsistence sphere, they could be used to pay for food if one wanted large amounts of food for a feast, or, to one's disgrace, if one had to buy to eat. But the rods could serve here only in large transactions; there were no small-change rods. Morally "upward," they came to be used in the marriage sphere, as earnest money or as a way of af- filiating the children of a *kem* marriage. It was "good," "successful," "strong- hearted" to convert upward, turning food into rods or rods into wives and daughters. Conversion between spheres increased the respect for and fear of one party to the transaction and lowered the respect for and fear of the other. In the views of buyer and seller and everyone else, no food could totally make up for conversion from rods down to food. This restricted the power of brass-rod money to organize or reorganize social relationships or economic organization.

Modern money in conjunction with British law changed the situation. The British brought peace, hence security in travel instead of death or enslavement, and therefore an expansion of the area and volume of trade. Peace and a "national Nigerian" economy connected with world markets led to the export of Tiv-produced foodstuffs and provided a way of earning modern multipurpose money. The British outlawed exchange marriage (it smacked of slavery in British eyes); furthermore, seeing the brass rods as "money," the British withdrew brass rods and substituted their own multipurpose money.

Exchange marriages outlawed, all marriages became *kem* and had to stay *kem*. Multipurpose money had to be substituted for brass rods in contracting a *kem* marriage and in *kemming* the offspring. The institutionalized moral boundaries between the spheres were destroyed. Money received in payment for food sold to traders for export from Tivland was the *only* means of payment to use both in the intermediate cattle-magic sphere and in the highest marriage sphere. Tiv efforts to order European money and goods into a fourth and "morally lowest" sphere failed. The markets-and-money of British rule have certainly changed the Tiv system of marriage. It is now possible for a man to sell subsistence goods and buy prestige goods and *kem* wives with money. There has been a loss of the order, ranking, and unity in the kinship-marriage system on which Tiv political, judicial, and social as well as economic life was based. The "price" of marriage has been inflated and the Tiv feel degraded at having to "sell" their daughters and "buy" their wives. It is ironic that the British efforts to stop processes which they regarded as slavery and the buying and selling of people has led the Tiv to think of themselves as forced by the British to buy and sell people.

## Similar Cases

Similar but worse problems arose in east Africa as a consequence of the same substitution of multipurpose money for cattle in the marriage systems. Paternal authority at home and the kin-group management of the herds was undermined. Though the men who migrated to the cities found they could contract a marriage with their earnings, these were not, however, proper marriages. The lines between marriage, liaisons, and prostitution became blurred. The role of marriage in forming clan alliances was destroyed for the migrants and much weakened for those who remained at home.[3]

Modern money has likewise been disintegrating the political structure of the Kapauku. About 1960 the Dutch began building an airstrip near their lands. Young Kapauku took construction jobs and used Dutch multipurpose

---

[3]Richard C. Thurnwald, *Black and White in East Africa: the Fabric of a New Civilization.*

money to finance their own rise within the Kapauku system. No longer needing to borrow—debts declined by three-fourths—the young no longer feared their elders and the elders were no longer able to exercise authority. Again, as in the case of the Tiv, there is irony—the Dutch had wanted to build their control upon the power and authority of the old political system that Dutch money had weakened.[4]

Wherever European multipurpose money has gone, it has had an impact on the nonwestern societies into which it has been introduced. This has been the case in India and Indonesia, for example, as well as in Africa and Oceania.[5]

---

[4]Pospisil, *The Kapauku*, p. 27.

[5]The literature is voluminous. For India see the citations in Chapter III (Bailey, Epstein, Neale, Beidelman) and Malcolm Darling, *The Punjab Peasant in Prosperity and Debt*, 4th edition. For Indonesia, see Clifford Geertz, *Agricultural Involution: The Process of Ecological Change in Indonesia*, and J. H. Boeke, *Economics and Economic Policy of Dual Societies* (Parts I & II).

# IX

## MONEY, PRICES, AND CREDIT

### Money and Prices

After any two-way transfer of goods one can compute a ratio of what is transferred by one party to what is transferred by the other party and call the ratio a price. When in our economy we transfer a good or perform a service and receive money or the promise of money, then we say that the money, which is made equivalent to the good or service by the two-way transfer of good or service for money, is the price of the good or service. An economist will say that the price of any one good can be expressed as the amount of any other good for which it will exchange; and it has been said by economists that money is a "veil" which disguises the "real" prices of goods and services in terms of each other. It is true that we could express all prices in terms of bushels of wheat or pounds of rice rather than in dollars or francs. We could do so in our present economic system by dividing every other money price by the money price of a pound of rice.

The statements that a 1-pound can of tomatoes costs $.30 and a 2-pound box of rice costs $1.75 can be restated by saying a 1-pound can of tomatoes costs .171 pounds of rice. We could express prices this way but we do not do so because we use dollars and francs, not bushels of wheat or pounds of rice, in which to keep our accounts and make our payments.

The observer of Trobriand society could make similar computations and call them prices. Noting that 1 head load of yams from inland villages elicits a return gift of 3 to 5 pounds of fish, the observer could say that the "price" of 1 head load of yams was 3 to 5 pounds of fish or he could quote the price of 3 to 5 pounds of fish as "1 head load of yams." He could thus "prove" that Trobrianders "also had prices," but to phrase the transactions between inland and coastal villages in terms of price adds nothing that we do not already know to our knowledge of how Trobrianders deal with each other. The prices so quoted are not meaningfully equivalent to our prices—consider the housewife's reaction at the supermarket to a price quotation on the can of "one can for 26¢ or 43¢ or somewhere in between."

In commercialized society, quoting a ratio in terms of money price is important because we can, and do, compare the price quoted by one seller with that quoted by another. We compare the price of one kind of item with the price of another kind—the price of a composition roof with the price of a tiled roof. We also compare the prices of unlike goods when deciding what we want to spend our money on. We compare the price of liquor for making cocktails with the price of new kitchen curtains because we can use our money income for either purpose. But the Trobriander could not compare the vague price ratios of fish and yams at two coastal villages and decide where to exchange gifts, because he had only one trading partner at one coastal village. To compute price or exchange ratios for Trobriand Islanders would be a highly misleading procedure because it would imply that the ratios had the same significance for Trobrianders that money prices have in a commercial society. In writing about bridewealth, Dalton has put the case against using our terminology of pricing: "To call a cat a quadruped, and then to say that because cats and dogs are both quadrupeds, I shall call them all cats, does not change the nature of cats. Neither does it confuse dogs; it merely confuses the reader. . . . When markets and Western money are absent, digging sticks are tools, not capital, and brides are not priced."[1]

## Money, Prices, and Costing

In a commercial economy a business firm buys all its inputs—raw materials and semifinished goods, labor, fuel and power, land, buildings, machinery—at a money cost on the markets for the various inputs. With all inputs available on markets at a price, and most inputs available only by paying the price, it is not only possible but also essential for the firm to make calculations of costs. The firm must know whether receipts from sales will cover its money outlays—if the receipts do not, the firm will have to go out of business. Where some of the inputs are already owned by the business, it is still important to the business to calculate the costs of these owned inputs in order to find out whether the profits—the difference between outlays and receipts—could be increased by selling the owned inputs and then buying or renting others at current prices to replace them.

Money as a unit of account *and* as a means of payment is vital to the

[1]George Dalton, "Bridewealth and Brideprice," *American Anthropologist* (June, 1966) 68:732-738, reprinted in George Dalton, *Economic Anthropology and Development: Essays on Tribal and Peasant Economies*. The quotation is from *American Anthropologist*, pp. 733-734 and 737, or from the reprint, pp. 195 and 200.

commercialized business concern. But money is not a vital consideration when inputs are not bought. A peasant family using its own land and labor and seeds from one harvest to another will be richer or poorer as the price of any product it sells rises or falls, but the peasant family will not be bankrupt —and therefore be unable to continue farming—if the prices fall because there are no money outlays for the land, labor, and seeds used. The fall in price will not even be a good indication of changes in the peasant family's standard of living. If two-thirds of the output of a peasant family are consumed within the household and one-third sold, a fall of 50 percent in the price received for the sold output will reduce the standard of living by only one-sixth; and a doubling of the price will make possible an increase in consumption of only one-sixth.

## Money and the Level of Prices

The relationship between the quantity of a money (the number of dollars in paper money, coins, and bank demand deposits; the number of shells; or the number of cows) and prices, or the value of the money in payment or exchange, has been expressed in an Equation of Exchange:

$$MV = PT, \quad \text{or} \quad P = MV/T$$

In this equation $M$ stands for the quantity of Money; $V$ for the Velocity of circulation, meaning the number of times, on the average, that a piece of money is used in payment during a period; $P$ for the level of Prices, or the average price of all goods sold; and $T$ for the number of Transactions, or the number of sales made during that period. Logically, the equation is a definition, a bit of circular reasoning. Both $MV$ and $PT$ represent the total amount of money paid over during a period. $M$, the quantity of money, multiplied by $V$, the average number of times each unit of the money is used, is the total amount paid during, say, a year. $P$, the average price of each transaction, multiplied by the number of transactions $(T)$, is also the total amount of money paid during the year. If we look at the other form of the equation, the average price $(P)$ is computed as the total amount of money paid ($M$ multiplied by $V$), divided by the number of times money is paid over $(T)$. It is argued that in commercialized economies the number of sales $(T)$ does not change greatly over a short period of time, nor does the average number of times each piece of money changes hands $(V)$; so that it can be said that the average price of items sold $(P)$ depends on the quantity of money $(M)$.

The causal sequence, more money causing higher prices, appears true enough of the sixteenth and seventeenth centuries when silver was flowing in from the New World. It also seems true of events in Germany in 1923 when the government was printing vast quantities of paper money and prices were rising hourly. The same statistical correlation holds for other periods, but it is possible that for some other periods $M$ might have depended on $P$. More money may have been a response to demands for more money to finance transactions in a situation in which prices were tending to rise for other reasons. It is true in these situations that if more money were not created, prices could not rise; but it also seems consistent with the history of money that if more money had not been created in the usual way, then people would have found other ways of creating more money—that is, invented more means of acceptable payment.

Whatever the causal sequence in any particular case, the relationships which the Equation of Exchange does emphasize are these: that more money must be associated either with (a) higher prices, (b) more transactions, or (c) less frequent use of each money item.

The association of (more or less) money with (higher or lower) prices has already been discussed. The association with the number of transactions ($T$ in the Equation of Exchange) also requires discussion.

One cause of an increase in the number of transactions has been that more things are produced for which money is paid. For instance, during the last third of the nineteenth century the output of industry and agriculture grew more than the number of money units of coin and paper money and demand deposits, all of which were linked to the quantity of gold in the world, and most prices fell.

The number of transactions may also increase because more kinds of transaction involve the use of money—a change called monetization. For instance, when tenants start paying money for the use of land instead of turning over a share of the actual, physical product, the tenants need money for these rental payments (transactions) that did not exist before. Similarly, when work is performed by wage labor rather than by kinsmen cooperating, as happened after the Pioneers conquered Central Africa, more money is needed for the increased number of wage payments (transactions).

More goods sold, or more obligations created and fulfilled, means either that the number of units of the money must rise ($M$ must increase), or that the frequency with which each money unit is used must rise ($V$ must increase), or that the number of units of the money used in each transaction must fall ($P$ must decrease). When the quantity of money grows no faster than the increased need for money as production grows or as more kinds of transaction are monetized, the price level remains about the same. Thus limiting the quantity of money tends to keep the price level stable.

There are several ways in which the quantity of a money ($M$) may be limited. It can be limited by the difficulty of making or finding more of the actual, physical item. Money made of precious metals has been limited in quantity by their scarcity in nature and the difficulties of mining them. Shells in the interior of New Guinea are limited in supply by the need to trade with coastal areas to get them. Other items which have been used as money have been limited in quantity because there are "offtakes" to other than money uses. For example, during and just after the First and Second World Wars cigarettes and chocolate bars served as means of payment; Germany in 1946 was said to be on a "Lucky Strike standard." The supply of cigarettes and chocolate bars by United States occupation troops would have increased the quantity of these "monies" enormously but for the fact that many recipients of these monies used them for nonmonetary purposes (smoking and eating) and so reduced the quantity of money at the same time that the soldiers were increasing it.

Paper money and bank-deposit money are not limited by any difficulty of finding or making. Enormous quantities of the paper money can be easily produced by modern printing presses, and enormous numbers of dollar or pound promises acceptable in payment can be made available by banks' exchanging of their own (demand deposit) promises for the unacceptable (to others) promises of people and other businesses (see Chapter 6). What limits the number of dollars in the United States or of pounds in Britain is the policies of the monetary authorities. The treasuries do not print money as the governments need it but instead tax or borrow from others. Insofar as they borrow from banks, there would be no limit on the money created; but most modern governments try to limit their borrowings from banks. Central banks of countries may try to make it difficult for banks to create more demand-deposit money by forcing adverse clearings on the banks and by refusing to accept the deposits of the banks in payment of the adverse clearing balances, thereby forcing the banks to limit the number of demand-deposit promises they make.

Upon occasion the monetary authorities in a country have not limited the supply of paper and bank monies, but on the contrary have engaged in a continuing process of printing more paper money or allowing the banks to lend more and more without the restraint of adverse clearings. Such was the case in Germany in 1923, when the number of marks was increased so fast that prices rose hourly. The government actually began overprinting larger numbers on old pieces of paper in order to increase the supply of money more rapidly.

The history of the cowrie illustrates the effect of large increases in the quantity of a means of payment. Cowries came from the Maldive Islands in the Bay of Bengal. Their use as a money stuff dates back thousands of years in, among other places, south Asia, ancient Egypt, and China. They spread widely but slowly, for they began to be used in Sub-Saharan Africa perhaps a thousand years ago. In seventeenth-century Bengal they were small change indeed, 3,000 to 4,000 of them being valued at one silver rupee coin. But in Uganda around 1800, 2 shells would "purchase a woman" (whether this was a bridewealth payment or what an Arab trader gave for a slave is not clear).[2]

As more and more cowries flowed into world trade the value of cowries declined. By the eighteenth century the Indian merchants of Bengal had warehouses full of cowries. The European ships trading to the east picked up cowries as ballast and used them in trade in west Africa. What had been rare because the source was so distant became so common in Uganda by 1896 that 200 cowries were equated, for purposes of paying taxes, with 1 rupee. Five years later, when the government ceased accepting cowries in payment of taxes, it took 800 cowries to equal 1 rupee. Unlike the precious metals, which have been discovered in nature little faster than men have found uses for them, the availability of cowries increased far faster than their uses. Unlike the cigarette, which disappears in smoke, the cowrie will last, as measured by man's span, forever; there is no offtake by using it up. Unlike modern nations that issue currencies, the peoples of south Asia, China, and Africa had no means of limiting the influx of cowries. (European introduction of glass beads has had much the same effect on the value of aggry beads.)

The history of the value of cowries contrasts with the history of other items used as money. The raffia cloth of the Lele could be woven in quantity, but the idea that it was more dignified to borrow or receive the cloth than to weave it limited its quantity, as did the fact that the cloths wore out. The stone money of Yap did not wear out, but being brought by canoe from Pelew, 400 miles distant, where it was found, with many a canoe overturning and sinking, the number of stones on Yap increased but slowly. Cattle and pigs die at some age if not killed sooner—there is an offtake.

## Means of Payment and Changing Amounts of Payment

Quite typical of anthropological reports is a statement that the quantities of goods flowing one way and the quantities flowing the other way in trading-partner arrangements or in arrangements between people connected by kinship, marriage, or other forms of alliance are "fixed" or "customary." Recently anthropologists have been making the point that over a period of time the quantities flowing in one direction will increase or decrease relative to the quantities flowing in the other direction—the equivalencies will change. This kind of change certainly occurs when an area is flooded with an item, as was the case when cowries were transported as ballast to Africa. It must also occur when an item becomes appreciably scarcer relative to its uses than it has been. Thus if, through disease or enemy raids or rapid increase in human population, the number of cattle in a society declines compared to the number of marriages, then there must be, of logical necessity, either an increased turnover of cows and oxen or a decline in the number transferred at

---

[2]Marshall Sahlins, *Stone Age Economics*, pp. 185-230 and 277-314. The quoted phrases are from p. 220.

each marriage. Taking together the reports of customary equivalencies in two-way flows of goods and the reports of changing equivalencies, the evidence indicates that changes in the equivalencies take place slowly. Unlike what happens in a capitalist or market economy, where prices change daily in response to reports about conditions of crops and length of order books and to news of changes in central bank policy or the rates of interest banks are charging customers, the changes in "equivalent flows" in tribal societies take years.

Marshall Sahlins has argued that the reason for fixity and change in two-way flows of goods is that the flows of goods are a "vehicle of peace and alliance" and a "symbol of the transformation from separate to harmonious interests." In other words, the immediate self-interest of a barterer without other ties and fears gives way to a kind of self-interested "generosity" that overcomes existing or possible hostility between groups which are not otherwise bound by a higher authority capable of enforcing peace between the groups.* "Generosity"—which can be defined here as fear of the consequences of being seen as stingy—prevents trading partners from trying hard "to make the best deal possible." But in the longer run this same "generosity" will lead to changes in the quantity of a good flowing in one direction. If one of the trading partners comes to feel that the other is putting much less effort into providing the good than he himself is there may be "a translation from trading goods to trading blows."[3] To avoid such resentment—in order to maintain not only the two-way flow of goods but also to maintain peace—the trading partner who can give more easily will increase the size of his "gifts."

The use of a stuff as a referent for a money of account or standard of value may add an element of confusion to efforts to analyze changing equivalencies in flows of things (and people). One can continue to express bridewealth in cattle while actually transferring fewer cows and more iron hoes or goats—or more cows and fewer iron hoes and goats if the number of available cattle increases. This possibility raises a peculiar indeterminacy in discussions of money: Are goats-which-are-not-money substituted for cows-which-are-money? Or, if goats become a common means of payment, has the money supply been increased by the number of goats available? The questions are not too different from questions one could ask about monies in the earlier stages of the development of modern, multipurpose monies: Were Massachusetts bills of credit substitutes for Spanish silver dollars and English shillings and pounds? Or were they, as modern historians of money have treated them, additions to the supply of money? Actually, these questions become trouble-

---

*It may also be that constancy in the flow of goods in both directions lessens the probability of physical conflict by giving each side a feeling of security about what will happen.

[3]Sahlins, p. 302.

some only if one insists that there be *a* money—only *one* money. If one recognizes, as the medieval merchant certainly did, that there can be a *number* of monies, then the student of the history of money or of comparative money simply goes on to account for the various different uses of different monies—multipurpose and limited-purpose—among and within specific societies.

## Credit

Credit (a name for a variety of arrangements for paying a debt in the future) is closely related to money. In many situations credit is a good substitute for money. Credit occurs when one person or organization agrees to allow another to make payment in the future. The agreement and the debt often arise simultaneously, as with any loan, but an agreement can be made after the debt occurs. Examples of the latter in modern society are time allowed to pay a fine or overdue taxes, and in the African societies discussed in Chapter IV, time allowed the wife's kin group to return the cattle after she has run away, or time allowed the killer's kin to pay the bloodwealth.

Often the debtor agrees to do or pay something in addition to the original debt—money interest on a loan, the increase in the livestock lent. There are situations in which there is "no charge" for the credit—when a neighbor borrows a lawnmower, and when lend-lease aid passed from the United States to its allies in World War II (only the unused and undestroyed goods had to be paid for or returned after the war). There are other arrangements about which it is difficult to tell whether there is (or was) a "charge" for the delay in payment. For instance, during the Middle Ages the church forbade the collection of such a "charge" (interest was usury, which was the deadly sin of avarice). However, the exchange rate between different currencies fluctuated, and was not the same everywhere, while there were "service" costs in arranging payment of debts across distances and political boundaries. Whether in any particular instance the stated amount of the debt to be paid in the future included a surreptitious interest charge (as many believe was usual) or only best guesses about the proper exchange rate in the future and about service costs, only the Omniscient can know for sure.

What all these postponed payments have in common is some variant of the statement by one party, the creditor, that he will believe the statement of the debtor that the payment will be made.

Credit differs from money in two respects. First, one can extend credit (make a loan) in a nonmonetary form; and neither party need measure the credit extended in monetary terms. If one adds this sort of credit to the sort of credit advanced or measured in monetary terms the phenomenon of credit is universal. Wherever, and that seems to be just about everywhere, there are obligations to make payments in the future rather than right away, one says that credit occurs there.

Second, credit can be compared to and contrasted with money in terms of acceptability in payment. Whereas my bank may accept my promise to pay, and stores running charge accounts may accept promises to pay by their customers, third parties are unlikely to accept these promises. Conversely, a bank's promises to pay—in the form of a banknote or a demand deposit—are accepted by many third, fourth, and fifth parties. Crediting a bank—believing that it will pay on demand, and accepting promises of a bank to pay on demand—makes bank credit money. Credit and money thus indeed merge into one in the case of demand deposits at banks. But where the promise of one party is accepted by only one other party, credit diverges from money. Credit is money when the promise to pay is accepted as full and final payment; credit is not thought of as money when the promise to pay is accepted in anticipation of some other form of payment later replacing the promise.

# X

## MONIES

In this book I have not attempted to define "money" because "money" is not a logical idea, like the idea of "parent" which always and exactly means someone who has had a child. Neither have I attempted to say that a stuff is money if it has particular traits or functions and not a money if it does not have those traits or functions, because such an effort would require that some things with moneyish traits, but not all the ones selected, be ignored although they play important roles in some societies. Consider some instances:

An important trait of modern money is fungibility: the characteristic that any representation of a quantity of the money can always be substituted for any other representation of the same quantity. Were one to insist that "it isn't money if it isn't fungible," one could not discuss cattle as money because the Africans who make payments in cattle know and evaluate each cow, bull, and ox separately. Yet these same people use the idea of cattle to measure values (cattle are a standard of value), to express obligations (cattle are a standard of deferred payment), to make payments, and to store wealth. The higher-valued shells of the Kapauku do not have exact equivalents in lower denomination shells. There are fairly regular equivalencies, but the shells are not entirely fungible.

If one were to insist that money be a medium of exchange, then one would have to say that the ghost monies of medieval Europe and the "skins" of the North American fur trade were not money although they were standards of value and, as expressions of obligations, they were both stores of value and standards of deferred payment.

And so through every trait and function one might wish to say is a necessary aspect of money.

What seems common to all historical and comparative studies of money is

that the stuffs or processes discussed have at least one of these two characteristics: (1) they are used to make several kinds of payments, and, if a stuff, a
particular item of the stuff is used more than once in making payments; and
(2) they serve to measure, in some sense, the value of some other things,
processes, or events. In fact, all stuffs or processes that have been called
money appear to have both these characteristics. But beyond these two
characteristics it is probably impossible to make any generalization.

In thinking about money it is best to think in the plural—about monies. It is
also best to think, not about money in the abstract, as having some universal
role in social and economic life, but to think about how each money fits into
the social, political, and economic structures of the society which used that
money. A money may be essential to livelihood, as it is in the industrialized
world. A money may be a nice thing to get and use but not be essential to life,
as is the case in many peasant societies. Or a money may be essential to social
relationships, having a vital role in the functioning of marriage systems and
systems of handling disputes.

Money is a powerful social device. It allows people to substitute a payment
in money for the performance of an action. It permits people to compare
quantitatively one thing with another, in terms of money values. It permits
people to compare quantitatively, in money values, things with events or
performances. If I do not deliver grain or foreign exchange on a futures
contract I can deliver money instead. If I do not want to kill one of your clan
in revenge I can accept money. I can compare a herd of cows to a skyscraper,
and either with scything a field of hay or with an operation performed by a
surgeon. Any of these I can compare with the risk of a shipwreck in New
York harbor. I can even compare my wife's difficulties in feeding pigs with
the pleasures of having carnal knowledge of your wife.

Money can induce performance, and it can be used to regulate performance. People will work for money or allow others to use their property for
money. Managements can evaluate the performance of subordinates by measuring inflows and outflows of money, and can bring about improved performance by the award and deprivation of money.

Monies have not had the same effects everywhere. The most powerful
money is our modern multipurpose money. Other monies have had lesser
effects. There was not much one could do with money in ninth-century
Europe. The power of money in the form of shells in Oceania was focused
narrowly upon women and pigs; and, in the form of cows in Africa, upon
women and violence. In sixteenth- and seventeenth-century Europe the power of money was focused upon long-distance trade (as much of the power of
money had been so focused in the medieval urban economy) and also upon
securing the power of the emerging central governments. In nineteenth-
century western Europe and North America the power was focused upon
marshaling the natural and human resources of the world for building im-

mensely productive, privately owned, inanimately powered modern industry and transport. In twentieth-century Soviet Russia it has been directed to assuring the success of a centrally planned program of industrial development and social transformation. In twentieth-century America women have used the "canned freedom" it gives to alter radically their relationships with men. With money, one can move a thousand miles and live successfully among strangers.

If we can harness the electrobiochemical processes to slot machines, money may even yet buy happiness.

# SOME REMARKS ON THE LITERATURE

The reader interested in pursuing the comparative study of money will not find many works on the subject specifically, but will find a great deal of material bearing on the subject in a wide variety of sources. The literature in economics, anthropology, and history dealing with money—to say nothing of the associated topics of trade and markets—is so extensive that no obvious listing can be given. The few suggestions made in this essay must be largely a matter of personal taste and experience; and the books discussed here, and others not mentioned but listed in "References and Bibliography," are ones this writer likes and has found clear or informative.

Anyone interested in any aspect of money needs to understand the most important money—modern multipurpose money. Sir Dennis Robertson's *Money* is a first-class short introduction, with a British bias. Lester V. Chandler's *The Economics of Money and Banking* is an excellent text, focusing on the United States system.

On the other side, it is important to grasp ways in which nonmarket and nonmonetized societies have provided for the production and distribution of the means of livelihood so that one does not "read money and markets into" other systems. For nonmarket systems in history a reader might start with Henri Frankfort, *The Birth of Civilization in the Near East*. For analyses of a range of nonmarket societies, try Chapters 1-12 in Karl Polanyi, Conrad M. Arensberg, and Harry W. Pearson, editors, *Trade and Market in the Ancient Empires* (often not easy reading).

The literature on primitive nonmarket economies might be sampled in C. Daryll Forde, *Habitat, Economy and Society*, covering a number of primitive societies, or in Bronislaw Malinowski's *Coral Gardens and Their Magic*, an intensive study of a single Melanesian society. *Coral Gardens*, along with

Malinowski's *Argonauts of the Western Pacific*, may be considered the beginning of economic anthropology. Another good book to start with is Paul and Laura Bohannan, *Tiv Economy*, or Chapters 13, 14, and 15 in Paul Bohannan's text, *Social Anthropology*.

To read with understanding in the history of money or about money in primitive and peasant societies requires at least a rough idea of the social system and economic organization of the society in which a money is used. It is this need for context which reduces the usefulness of the only two extensive comparative surveys (Quiggin's *Survey of Primitive Money* and Einzig's *Primitive Money*). Quiggin's *Survey* is strong in describing the physical, zoological, and botanical characteristics of the many money stuffs reported in the anthropological literature up to 1947. She also provides a good many examples of the particular transactions in which the money stuffs were used. The book is, however, weak in that it gives little of the social and economic context of the societies in which the money stuffs were used. It is a useful source if one wants to know the zoology of the cowrie which lived in the shell or where the sources of a money stuff were located. It is also useful if one wants citations of other sources where fuller information is given. Einzig's book covers much the same literature as Quiggin's but in addition has a great deal more material drawn from historical sources. His bibliography is much longer than Quiggin's and he reports on more recent literature. Like Quiggin, Einzig concentrates on the money stuff. He is weaker than Quiggin on the physical nature of the stuffs but often provides some idea about how the money fitted into the social structure. However, the accounts of the societies are minimal and sometimes omitted. His theoretical section, some two hundred pages long, is perhaps more useful to a reader as an example of an economist's approach than it is as an analysis of the roles and significance of money at different times and places. The theoretical section is, however, more sophisticated than the treatment of primitive and early monies in standard works on money and banking. Both Quiggin and Einzig are best treated as useful starting points or as sources for further reading on topics on which one has already done some reading.

The literature in the field of economic anthropology is growing. During the past fifteen years there has been a continuing fight between a group called "the formalists" and a group called "the substantivists." The fight has been over how to state and how to interpret economic phenomena, but has not yet impinged much on the subject of money (the dispute has focused on rationality, trade, and markets) and it is probably safe to study ethnographies without worrying over the dispute. While a substantivist myself, I have found no difficulty in using descriptions by people on both sides. If one wants to read this part of the literature, it culminated in an article by George Dalton in *Current Anthropology* (1969), with replies in that and subsequent issues. The references therein are more than sufficient to find out what has been said and how high feelings run. To understand the dispute, however, one should read the articles by Humphreys on the thought of Karl Polanyi and by Kaplan on the background, in economics, to the dispute.

The best "readers" in economic anthropology are two edited by George Dalton. Dalton is a "substantivist," but the selection is wide. A "formalist" selection is to be found in the reader edited by LeClair and Schneider. Two short paperbacks introduce the reader to economic anthropology—Nash's *Primitive and Peasant Economic Systems* and Belshaw's *Traditional Exchange and Modern Markets* (my slightly preferred one)—and are probably a better place to start than is Herskovits's *Economic Anthropology*, which was the first book to attempt a general survey of the field. More sophisticated, but essential reading for anyone going on in the field of economic anthropology, is *Themes in Economic Anthropology*, edited by Raymond Firth (who ranks second in time to and perhaps co-equal in influence with Malinowski as a founder of economic anthropology). Also at a higher level of sophistication are the works of Karl Polanyi, some of which are usefully brought together in Dalton's collection, *Primitive, Archaic and Modern Economies*. See especially Chapter 8, "The Semantics of Money-Uses."

On money in European (including American) civilization, one might add to the citations in Chapter V Bloch's *Feudal Society* for medieval society and economy, and Chapter 8 ("Natural Economy or Money Economy: A Pseudo-Dilemma") of his *Land and Work in Medieval Europe*. For the eighteenth and nineteenth centuries one might sample the books listed below by Pressnell, Cameron, Feis, and Hammond; and for the twentieth century the book by Ferris, which is clear, entertaining, and sophisticated.

# REFERENCES AND BIBLIOGRAPHY

Bailey, F. G. *Caste and the Economic Frontier*. Manchester: Manchester University Press, 1957.

Barber, William J. *The Economy of British Central Africa*. Stanford, Cal.: Stanford University Press, 1961.

Beidelman, Thomas O. *A Comparative Analysis of the Jajmani System* (Monograph #7 of the Association for Asian Studies). Locust Valley, N.Y.: J. J. Augustin, 1959.

Belshaw, Cyril S. *Traditional Exchange and Modern Markets*. Englewood Cliffs, N.J.: Prentice-Hall, 1965.

Bloch, Marc. *Feudal Society*. Chicago: University of Chicago Press, 1961 (translated from the French by L. A. Manyon).

Bloch, Marc. *Land and Work in Medieval Europe*. Berkeley: University of California Press/London: Routledge and Kegan Paul, 1967 (translated from the French by J. E. Anderson).

Boeke, J. H. *Economics and Economic Policy of Dual Societies* (Parts I and II). New York: Institute of Pacific Relations, 1946.

Bohannan, Paul. "The Impact of Money on an African Subsistence Economy." *The Journal of Economic History* (1959) 19:491-503; reprinted in Dalton, *Tribal and Peasant Economies*, pp. 123-135.

Bohannan, Paul. *Social Anthropology*. New York/London: Holt, Rinehart & Winston, 1963.

Bohannan, Paul, and Laura Bohannan. *Tiv Economy*. Evanston: Northwestern University Press, 1965.

Bohannan, Paul, and George Dalton, editors. *Markets in Africa*. Garden City: Doubleday & Company, 1965.

Cameron, Rondo, editor. *Banking and Economic Development: Some Lessons of History*. New York/London/Toronto: Oxford University Press, 1972.

Cameron, Rondo, editor. *Banking in the Early Stages of Industrialization*. New York/London/Toronto: Oxford University Press, 1967.

Chandler, Lester V. *The Economics of Money and Banking*, 5th edition. New York/Evanston/London: Harper & Row, 1969.

Chayanov, A. V. *The Theory of Peasant Economy*, edited by Daniel Thorner, Basile Kerblay, and R. E. F. Smith. Homewood, Ill.: Richard D. Irwin (for the American Economic Association), 1966.

Cipolla, Carlo M. *Money, Prices, and Civilization in the Mediterranean World, Fifth to Seventeenth Century*. New York: Gordian Press, 1967.

Dalton, George. "Bridewealth and Brideprice." *American Anthropologist* (June, 1966) 68:732-738; reprinted in Dalton, *Economic Anthropology and Development*, pp. 193-201.

Dalton, George. *Economic Anthropology and Development: Essays on Tribal and Peasant Economies*. New York/London: Basic Books, 1971.

Dalton, George, editor. *Economic Development and Social Change: The Modernization of Village Communities*. Garden City, N.Y.: The Natural History Press (for The American Museum of Natural History), 1971.

Dalton, George, editor. *Primitive, Archaic, and Modern Economies: Essays of Karl Polanyi*. Boston: Beacon Press, 1971 © 1968.

Dalton, George. "Primitive Money." *American Anthropologist* (1965) 67:44-65; reprinted in Dalton, *Economic Anthropology and Development*, pp. 167-192.

Dalton, George. "Theoretical Issues in Economic Anthropology" with "comments." *Current Anthropology* (February, 1969) 10:1:63-102; reprinted in Dalton, *Economic Anthropology and Development*, pp. 70-119.

Dalton, George, editor. *Tribal and Peasant Economies: Readings in Economic Anthropology*. Garden City, N.Y.: The Natural History Press (for The American Museum of Natural History), 1967.

Darling, Malcolm. *The Punjab Peasant in Prosperity and Debt*, 4th edition. New Haven: Human Relations Area Files, 1956 © 1947.

Dobb, Maurice. *Soviet Economic Development Since 1917*. London: Routledge & Kegan Paul, 1966.

Douglas, Mary. "The Lele—Resistance to Change," in Bohannan and Dalton, editors, *Markets in Africa*, pp. 183-213.

Douglas, Mary. "Raffia Cloth Distribution in the Lele Economy." *Africa* (1958) 29:109-122; reprinted in Dalton, *Tribal and Peasant Economies*, pp. 103-122.

Einaudi, Luigi. "The Theory of Imaginary Money from Charlemagne to the French Revolution," in Lane and Riemersma, editors, *Enterprise and Secular Change*, pp. 229-261.

Einzig, Paul. *Primitive Money: In Its Ethnological, Historical, and Economic Aspects*, 2nd edition. London/New York: Pergamon Press, 1966.

Epstein, T. Scarlett. *Economic Development and Social Change in South India*. Manchester: Manchester University Press, 1962.

Epstein, T. Scarlett. *South India: Yesterday, Today, and Tomorrow*. New York: Holmes and Meier, 1973.

Evans-Pritchard, E. E. *The Nuer*. Oxford: The Clarendon Press, 1940.

Feis, Herbert, editor. *Europe: the World's Banker, 1870-1914*. New York: W. W. Norton & Co., 1965; © 1930 by Yale University Press.

Ferris, Paul. *Men and Money*. Harmondsworth, Middlesex: Penguin Books, 1970.

Firth, Raymond, editor. *Themes in Economic Anthropology* (Association of Social Anthropologists Monograph #6). London/New York: Tavistock Publications, 1967.

Forde, C. Daryll. *Habitat, Economy and Society*, 3rd edition. London: Methuen & Co., 1939.

Frankfort, Henri. *The Birth of Civilization in the Near East*. Garden City, N.Y.: Doubleday & Company, 1956.

Geertz, Clifford. *Agricultural Involution: The Process of Ecological Change in Indonesia*. Berkeley: University of California Press, 1963.

Goldschmidt, Walter. *Kambuya's Cattle: The Legacy of an African Herdsman*. Berkeley/Los Angeles: University of California Press, 1969.

Gross, Ruth Below. *Money, Money, Money*, illustrated by Leslie Jacobs. New York/Toronto/London/Auckland/Sydney: Scholastic Book Services, n.d.

Hammond, Bray. *Banks and Politics in America, from the Revolution to the Civil War*. Princeton, N.J.: Princeton University Press, 1957.

Hawtrey, R. G. *The Gold Standard in Theory and Practice*, 5th edition. London/New York/Toronto: Longmans, Green & Co., 1947.

Herskovits, Melville J. *Economic Anthropology: A Study in Comparative Economics*. New York: Alfred A. Knopf, 1922. The earlier edition was entitled *The Economic Life of Primitive Peoples* (New York: Alfred A. Knopf, 1940).

Humphreys, S. C. "History, Economics, and Anthropology: The Work of Karl Polanyi," *History and Theory* (1969) 8:2:165-212.

Jasny, Naum. *The Soviet Economy During the Plan Era*. Stanford, Cal.: Stanford University Press, 1951.

Kaplan, David "The Formal-Substantive Controversy in Economic Anthropology: Reflections on Its Wider Implications." *Southwestern Journal of Anthropology* (Autumn, 1968) XXIV:3:228-251.

Lane, Frederic C., and Jelle C. Riemersma, editors. *Enterprise and Secular Change*. Homewood, Ill.: Richard D. Irwin, 1953.

LeClair, Edward E., Jr., and Harold K. Schneider, editors. *Economic Anthropology: Readings in Theory and Analysis*. New York: Holt, Rinehart & Winston, 1968.

Malinowski, Bronislaw. *Argonauts of the Western Pacific*. New York: E. P. Dutton & Co., 1961/London: Routledge & Kegan Paul, © 1935.

Malinowski, Bronislaw. *"Kula:* the Circulating Exchange of Valuables in the Archipelagoes of Eastern New Guinea," in Dalton, *Tribal and Peasant Economies*, pp. 187-194.

Malinowski, Bronislaw. "Tribal Economics in the Trobriands," in Dalton, *Tribal and Peasant Economies*, pp. 185-223.

Mason, Philip. *The Birth of a Dilemma*. London/New York/Toronto: Oxford University Press, 1958.

Middleton, John, and David Tait. *Tribes without Rulers*. New York: Humanities Press, 1958.

Nash, Manning. *Primitive and Peasant Economic Systems*. San Francisco: Chandler Publishing Company, 1966.

Neale, Walter C. *Economic Change in Rural India: Land Tenure and Reform in Uttar Pradesh, 1800-1955*. New Haven/London: Yale University Press, 1962.

Pirenne, Henri. *Economic and Social History of Medieval Europe*. New York: Harcourt, Brace and World, 1937.

Polanyi, Karl. *Dahomey and the Slave Trade: An Analysis of an Archaic Economy* (in collaboration with Abraham Rotstein). Seattle/London: University of Washington Press, 1966.

Polanyi, Karl, Conrad M. Arensberg, and Henry W. Pearson, editors. *Trade and Market in the Early Empires*. Glencoe, Ill.: The Free Press, 1957.

Pospisil, Leopold J. *The Kapauku Papuans of West New Guinea*. New York: Holt, Rinehart & Winston, 1965 © 1963.

Pressnell, L. S. *Country Banking in the Industrial Revolution*. Oxford: Clarendon Press, 1956.

Quiggin, A. Hingston. *A Survey of Primitive Money: The Beginning of Currency*. London: Methuen & Co., 1949.

Read, Margaret. "Migrant Labour in Africa and Its Effects on Tribal Life." *International Labour Review* (June, 1942) XLV:6:605-631.

Rigby, Peter. *Cattle and Kinship Among the Gogo: A Semi-Pastoral Society of Central Tanzania*. Ithaca, N.Y./London: Cornell University Press, 1969.

Robertson, Dennis. *Money*. Chicago: University of Chicago Press, 1959.

Sahlins, Marshall. *Stone Age Economics*. Chicago/New York: Aldine-Atherton, 1972.

Schneider, Harold K. *The Wahi Wanyaturu: Economics in an African Society* (Viking Fund Publications in Anthropology #48). New York: Wenner-Gren Foundation for Anthropological Research, 1970.

Sherman, Howard J. *The Soviet Economy*. Boston: Little, Brown & Co., 1969.

Spulber, Nicholas. *The Soviet Economy: Structure, Principles, Problems*. New York: W. W. Norton & Co., 1962.

Thurnwald, Richard C. *Black and White in East Africa: The Fabric of a New Civilization*. New York: The Humanities Press, 1950 © 1933.

Thurnwald, Richard C. "Pigs and Currency in Buin: Observations About Primitive Standards of Value and Economics." *Oceania* (1934) V:2:119-142; reprinted in Dalton, *Tribal and Peasant Economies*.

Van Roy, Edward. *Economic Systems of Northern Thailand, Structure and Change*. Ithaca, N.Y./London: Cornell University Press, 1971.

Wilson, Charles. *Mercantilism*. London: The Historical Association, 1958.

Wilson, Charles. "Treasures and Trade Balances: The Mercantilist Problem." *Economic History Review*, 2nd series (1949) II:152-161; reprinted in Lane and Riemersma, editors, *Enterprise and Secular Change*, pp. 337-349.

Wilson, Godfrey, and Monica Wilson. *An Essay on the Economics of Detribalization in Northern Rhodesia*. Livingston, N.R.: The Rhodes-Livingston Institute, 1941.

# INDEX